PRAYING THE PROVERBS

To Believe Your Way to Success

PRAYING ECCLESIASTES

To Avoid Trouble and Sin

PRAYING THE SONG OF SOLOMON

To Learn the Meaning of Love

PRAYING THE PROVERBS

To Believe Your Way to Success

PRAYING ECCLESIASTES

To Avoid Trouble and Sin

PRAYING THE SONG OF SOLOMON

To Learn the Meaning of Love

ELMER L. TOWNS

Destiny Image® Publishers, Inc.

P.O. Box 310
Shippensburg, PA 17257-0310

*"Speaking to the Purposes of God for This Generation
and for the Generations to Come"*

ISBN 978-0-7684-2316-7
0-7684-2316-3

For Worldwide Distribution
Printed in the U.S.A.

This book and all other Destiny Image, Revival Press, MercyPlace, Fresh Bread, Destiny Image Fiction, and Treasure House books are available at Christian bookstores and distributors worldwide.

1 2 3 4 5 6 7 8 9 10 / 10 09 08 07 06

For a U.S. bookstore nearest you, call
1-800-722-6774.

For more information on foreign distributors, call
717-532-3040.

Or reach us on the Internet:
www.destinyimage.com

ENDORSEMENTS

Elmer Towns is a personal friend of mine and we've traveled the world together. He is one of the most spiritual men I know and is eminently qualified to produce this book. Not only is he a biblical scholar in Greek and Hebrew so he can translate from the Hebrew, he is also a godly scholar who can lead the reader in their approach to God. I want every one of the thousands of workers involved in the Global Pastors Network to join me and pray the Proverbs, Ecclesiastes and Song of Solomon.

James O. Davis
Co-founder and President of Global Pastors Network

Elmer Towns' new book on how to pray the Proverbs, Ecclesiastes, and Song of Solomon is a journalistic breakthrough. Nothing like this has ever been done before. As a professor of Old Testament scriptures, I am amazed how accurately he developed his previous book, *How to Pray the Psalms*. Now, he has provided an even greater tool to help us pray with the wisdom of Solomon. Don't miss this unique, helpful and practical guide. It will expand your prayer life and strengthen your walk with God.

Dr. Ed Hindson
Professor of Old Testament
Liberty University

I met Elmer Towns 35 years ago and loved his enthusiasm for evangelism and church growth. However, Elmer has grounded his research in evangelism in the Word of God, specifically the original languages. That's why God has used him so greatly. Now he has used his knowledge of Hebrew to translate a wonderful book to help us know God and touch Him. *Praying the Proverbs* will bring us all closer to God; I recommend that all my friends use this book in their daily devotions.

C. Peter Wagner, Chancellor
Wagner Leadership Institute

TABLE OF CONTENTS

PRAYING THE PROVERBS
To Believe Your Way to Success

PRAYING ECCLESIASTES

To Avoid Trouble and Sin

PRAYING THE SONG OF SOLOMON
To Learn the Meaning of Love

PRAYING
THE PROVERBS
To Believe Your Way to Success

Introduction

You're holding in your hands a book that could change your life. If you will honestly pray the Proverbs it will help you live better. The theme might be "Believing your way to successful living."

God didn't include a lot of things in Proverbs. There is no plan of salvation, doctrine, Messianic predictions, and there is no plot. You'll get these topics in other books of the Bible.

There are no plots or storyline and no individuals identified by name in Proverbs, only Solomon (I believe the other named authors are other names for Solomon). Proverbs gets its points across by brief, one or two-line descriptions (character sketches) to illustrate proper living. These characters are not involved in stories or conversations with each other. You only get a fleeting glimpse of them throughout the book.

In the winter of 2004 and 2005 I translated Proverbs from the original language into modern English during my daily devotions. But I did more than turn Hebrew words into English; I transliterated each proverb into a prayer, then made it my intercession for that day. I translated the Proverbs to tie your prayer life to your everyday life. When you pray each proverb, you're asking God to help you believe your way to successful living. You're asking God to give you common sense so you can live by right principles.

So, pray your way through Proverbs so you can believe like God wants you to believe, and live like God wants you to live.

I wish you were beside me as I worked my way through this manuscript. I learned so much about the attitudes that God wants me to have toward life—and how to put each into action. Proverbs is so deep; we could spend our lifetime in this book and never exhaust its meanings.

As you read, may the Proverbs open up a new life for you. As you pray, may you touch God, but more importantly; may God touch you.

Sincerely yours in Christ,

Elmer Towns
Written from my home at the foot
of the Blue Ridge Mountains

WHAT ARE THE PROVERBS?

The Book of Proverbs is one of the five Old Testament books that is a part of wisdom literature, i.e., Proverbs, Job, Ecclesiastes, Song of Solomon and certainly the Psalms.

A proverb is a pithy saying, or brief popular saying that encapsulates a specific truth in two lines. Notice the word "verb" appears in proverbs, meaning it is an action sentence that contains truth.

Proverbs are usually expressed in catchy language. American proverbs or pithy sayings usually are one-line long, however, they are usually two-lines long in Scripture. A proverb usually has familiar truth that is popularly known and often repeated by the general population, yet it is expressed in simple metaphorical truth so that people may apply or honor its teaching.

The thrust of Proverbs is "apply your heart to wisdom, that you may gain understanding." This is another way of saying learn to think what is right, so you'll do what is right. The theme of Proverbs is "believing your way to successful living."

A proverb has the true wisdom that comes from the Lord. There is a ". . . wisdom of this world . . ." (1 Cor. 2:1-8; James 3:13,15) but that is not God's wisdom. Most Christians have identified true wisdom with Jesus Christ, He is the wisdom of God. The description of God's wisdom is seen in Proverbs 8:22-31 which says that wisdom is eternal (Prov. 8:22-26) just as Jesus Christ is eternal, "Jesus Christ the same yesterday, and today, and for ever" (Heb. 13:8 KJV). Wisdom also is responsible for the creation of all things (Prov. 8:27-29), just as Jesus Christ created all things (John 1:3; Col. 1:16). Again, wisdom is called the *beloved of God* (Prov. 8:30-31), and so is Jesus Christ (John 1:1,2; Col. 1:15,19). Therefore, when the Old Testament describes getting true wisdom, it is a New Testament picture of having Jesus Christ control your life.

Notice what is not included in Proverbs. It does not include the plan of salvation, nor does it exhort people to be converted. It doesn't have a Messianic prediction, nor does it teach doctrine. There are no miracles in Proverbs. God's plan for the Book of Proverbs was to give the reader God's perspective of what the older generations call "common sense." Therefore, Proverbs has good advice to direct the lives of both those who are not saved and those who have entered into God's covenant and desire to live for Him.

Solomon wrote approximately 3,000 proverbs (1 Kings 4:32), and this led to the popular idea that the 800 verses of Proverbs were the product of his hand. However, a correct interpretation of the Hebrew language reads, "The words of the wise for Solomon, the son of David, the king of Israel (Prov. 1:1)."

Instructions for Solomon When He Becomes King
(Prov. 1:1–9:18)

The section of Proverbs 1:1 to 9:18 includes instructions by David for Solomon as he became the king of Israel. Notice throughout this section that it is the instruction of the father David to his son Solomon. Also, you will find throughout the admonition "my son" which suggests David is telling Solomon how to conduct himself once he becomes king. The section also uses the pronoun in the *King James Version* "thy," "thee," "thou," "thine" and "thy mother," perhaps a reference to Bathsheba.

Proverbs by Solomon
(Prov. 10:1–19:19)

The second section of Proverbs, 10:1–19:19 are written by Solomon. Notice they begin "the proverbs by Solomon," and no longer refers to him in the third person, i.e., "he," "his," and "him." No longer does the author refer to "my son" as seen in the previous passage. This is because Solomon is now writing, rather than being written to. This second section is to direct the life of all God's people, not just for the young prince who was being prepared to become king of Israel.

Proverbs for Solomon
(Prov. 19:20–24:34)

This section begins with "my son" so these proverbs are again for Solomon. Notice the reference to "he," "him," and "his." These are the proverbs to guide Solomon when he becomes king.

The proverbs of the wise men under King Hezekiah are those that were found in the palace library that had been originally written by Solomon (Prov. 25:1). These men under Hezekiah's direction copied them by the inspiration of God and are included in Scripture. There is no question they were inspired of God, the question is how did they get to us? These proverbs were originally spoken by Solomon and were copied by his scribes or were actually penned by Solomon himself. They were placed in the royal library, and later added to the canon by scribes of Hezekiah.

Chapter 30 was written by Agur (Prov. 30:1) and chapter 31 was written by King Lemuel, other names for Solomon. Solomon wrote these, because the Talmud calls Solomon by six names: Solomon, Jedidiah, Koheleth, Son of Jakeh, Agur, and Lemuel.

The last section (Prov. 31:1-31) is the words of King Lemuel. The name Lemuel comes from *El* (which is Jehovah) and *Lem* (which means king, i.e., God's beloved king). This is Solomon himself because at his birth Solomon was called Jedidiah, *beloved of Jehovah* (2 Sam. 12:25).

DEFINITIONS

Father – refers to a teacher throughout the Book of Proverbs, and thus throughout the rest of Scripture (2 Kings 2:12; 6:21; 13:14; Judg. 17:10; 18:19).

Son – refers to a pupil (1 Sam. 3:6,16; 2 Kings 2:3,5,7,15).

Fool – refers to hard-headed people who reject sound counsel. In fact, they are self-centered in that they think they know everything. Fools are pictured as spiritual rebels against God. Other words for fool are: sinner, wicked, or hypocrite (Prov. 3:33, 28:4,28; 29:2). There are three Hebrew words that are translated *fool*.

1. *evil* – describes a person with careless habits of mind or body (Prov. 7:22; 10:8; 13:21; 11:29; etc.).
2. *kesil* – means dense, unresponsive or one who refuses to learn. This appears 49 times in Proverbs (Prov. 1:22,32; 3:35; etc.).
3. *nabal* – a vulgar person who expresses a rebellious nature. Occurs 3 times (Prov. 17:7,21; 30:22).

Strange Woman – is from the two Hebrews words *zarah* and *mokriah*. Technically, she was not just a sinning Israelite woman, but also referred to as an alien: a Gentile woman. When a man is told not to associate with the strange woman, the Bible is advocating he must not only demonstrate personal purity, but also religious purity because the strange woman separates him from the covenant purpose of God if she is a Gentile. Today,

19

those who have sex with a whorish woman not only sin against their body, but they sin against God. I have called this woman a trollop.

Wisdom – this word is the truth of God applied to life, i.e., those principles that are right that help a person live right.

The key word of Proverbs is *wisdom*, the theme is "get wisdom so you can think your way to successful living."

There are six Hebrew words translated *wisdom*.

1. *chokmah* – which is translated 42 times as true wisdom, or that which is consistent with all that God decrees. This is right principles upon which all the laws of God are established.

2. *binah* – which is discernment or discrimination (Prov. 23:4) and in 12 of the *King James Version* passages is rendered "understanding."

3. *lab* – is the word also translated heart. This word is also translated wisdom (Prov. 10:21; 11:12; 15:21; 19:8), meaning wisdom that we know innately.

4. *ermah* – which is translated wisdom but also means shrewdness (Prov. 1:4; 8:5).

5. *sakal* – translated good sense or what is sometimes called common sense (Prov. 1:3).

6. *sekel* – is translated insight or understanding (Prov. 3:4; 12:8; 15:15; 16:22; 23:9).

Instruction – means to admonish or discipline a student and sometimes it means to punish or chasten when a student is wrong.

Words – means the sayings or thoughts of a person. The term *words* is translated from *im* or *ah* and represents what a person has learned.

Simple – means a person who is guileless, unsuspecting, or untaught (Prov. 7:7; 8:5; 9:4; 16:14,15; 19:25; 21:1; 22:3; 27:12). It doesn't mean dumb or stupid because those terms suggest that the person can't learn. However, the simple can learn and that's why the Book of Proverbs wants the simple to be instructed. The simple who refuse instruction becomes a fool.

Interpretation – means to explain the meaning of the point of what is said.

Fear – does not mean to be afraid or scare, but rather to reverence. Fear is reverential trust, which is a term of salvation. It is used 14 times in Proverbs as in "fearing the Lord."

Proverbs

CHAPTER 1
A Father Teaches—Be Wise

The proverbs for Solomon, King of Israel,
The son of David.

Lord, help me learn and obey Your requirements,
So I will always know what to do.
Give me all the wisdom I need,
So I will always be fair and impartial.
Help me teach those who don't know
All they need to know and do.
Help me carefully listen and learn,
And become more understanding
So I will always do the right thing.
Help me gain much counsel from the wise
So I can become a smart person,
And learn to understand things that are difficult.

Lord, I know all wisdom is in You,
Help me understand Your ways
And not be rebellious to despise Your direction.

Help me listen to You as a father
And obey You as a mother.
May others see Your principles guiding my life
And may they glorify Your beauty.

Lord, help me resist the temptation of sinners
And not give in to them.
When sinners want me to make illegal money
And take advantage of innocent people,
May I resist their temptation.
Because when I destroy the lives of other people,
I am really condemning my own life.
Even when sinners promise me exorbitant riches
And a wealthy home and furnishings
And they promise to share their wealth with me,

Lord, I remember You said, "Stay away from them,"
"Don't be like them or obligate yourself to them,"
For they really intend to break every law
And suck the life out of innocent people.
Every plan they make to catch someone
Snares them into their own addiction.
And the happiness they plan to steal from others
They destroy any chance of enjoying it on the altar of their greed.

Lord, I see the eyes of honesty
Weeping over the crimes she sees in life—
Honesty crying for crimes to be punished.
And I hear the voice of honesty
Crying in the empty courts of justice,
"How long will evil run rampant?"
Honesty cries, "How long will skeptics be skeptical?"
"How long will rebels hate God's ways?"

Lord, You call us to return to You;
You promise to pour Your Spirit on us;
You promise to teach us Your ways.
Lord, when You call to the rebel,
You also stretch out Your hand to him;
But the rebel not only rejects Your ways,
He determines to do the exact opposite

And completely rejects all You stand for.
Therefore, You will turn Your back when he is punished,
You will say, "You got what you wanted."
Then the rebel will be scared to death
And the consequences of his sin rip him apart
When he cries out in anguish.
He shall cry out for mercy but not get it;
He shall seek You but You'll not be found.
There is no second chance in Hell,
Because the rebel hated Your way of life
And would not listen and learn from You.
He rejected Your plans for his life
And refused to do what You wanted him to do.
Therefore, he shall bear the consequences of his sin.
He shall suffer the misery he gives others;
His vile trespass shall be his own punishment.

Lord, because Your children turning to You
Shall be proof that the wicked could have repented;
Lord, Your prosperity on the righteous
Should have warned the wicked to change.

But Lord, those who listen and learn from Your instructions
Shall be safe in Your presence,
And shall be delivered from evil.
Amen

CHARACTER SKETCH:

The Fool

In our contemporary society, we seem to put some fools on a pedestal. In my day I laughed at Lou Costello of the Abbott and Costello team because he did foolish things. In the same way, I laughed at Jerry Lewis of the Lewis and Martin comedy team because he too did foolish things. Then we all laughed at the Three Stooges and the team of Laurel and Hardy. These men were not foolish and stupid; they only pretended to get us to laugh.

However, the Bible identifies a fool differently. A fool is a man or woman who refuses to follow common sense, who refuses to obey the rules, and who refuses to do the things we call wise. The fool has rejected God, "The fool has said in his heart, 'There is no God'" (Ps. 14:1). This person is described, "They hated knowledge and did not choose the fear of the Lord" (Prov. 1:29). Rather than doing the right thing, the fool would rather do selfish things, or do what makes him happy, or what satisfies the flesh. Because the fool marches to his own drumbeat, he hates rules and laws. The fool wants to do things that transgress the law (Prov. 10:23; 13:19; 29:27).

There is another thing that is foolish about a fool, they trust themselves rather than God's way of doing things (Prov. 1:7,29). As a result, the fool justifies everything in his own eyes (Prov. 12:15); but in contrast, the wise man will listen to counsel and will do what wise men tell him to do. When a person trusts only himself, he is arrogant (Prov. 21:24).

The fool is a cross between two types of contemporary people. First, the fool is dumb, which is like a person who is ignorant and does not know what to do, or how to do things, or why things are done right. Most dumb people can learn and become smart, but a fool probably won't learn.

There's a second problem. The fool is selfish to the extreme. They want attention, physical comfort, and they want things. They are selfish to the point of being obnoxious, but they are not willing to take the proper steps to get what they desperately want in life. They are blind to their selfish addiction, and what keeps them from their life's goal. A fool may be a good person who everyone likes, when in actuality some only tolerate them, or use them. They are fools because they fool themselves.

What Can We Know About a Fool?

First, we know that a fool does not prize living right, i.e., doing right or good things rightly. A fool follows his own selfish impulse. "A desire accomplished is sweet to the soul, But [it is] an abomination to fools to depart from evil" (Prov. 13:19). According to this verse, fools do not take pleasure in profitable accomplishments, i.e., "a desire accomplished." That means they do not find fulfillment in the craftsmanship of their own excellence.

Second, a fool justifies his sinful and selfish pursuits by finding fun in evil things. "To do evil [is] like sport to a fool" (Prov. 10:23). When the foolish man is caught breaking one of the Ten Commandments, he justifies himself, "I was just kidding" or "I was just fooling around."

Third, fools make fun of those who live righteously and they laugh with those who break the law. When it's pointed out that they're breaking the law, they just laugh to say, "It is nothing." The Bible says, "Fools mock at sin" (Prov. 14:9).

Fourth, a fool thinks he can hire people to be good for him, or a fool thinks that he can hire a wise man to make good decisions for him, or to do the right thing for him. "Why [is there] in the hand of a fool the purchase price of wisdom, since [he has] no heart [for it?]" (Prov. 17:16).

Fifth, a fool won't listen to good advice. There is a high price for becoming wise; it takes study, determination, and self-discipline. The one who gets through college or attains education has paid a price to learn. But not the fool; "Wisdom [is] too lofty for a fool" (Prov. 24:7). Also, "The fear of the Lord [is] the beginning of knowledge, [But] fools despise wisdom and instruction" (Prov. 1:7).

26

Sixth, a fool is emotionally undisciplined. He has never learned to hold his temper. Because his emotions control him, problems control a fool. "A fool's wrath is known at once, but a prudent [man] covers shame" (Prov. 12:16). A fool will lose his temper, "The discretion of a man makes him slow to anger, and his glory [is] to overlook a transgression" (Prov. 19:11).

And also, a fool cannot control his tongue. He says the right thing at the wrong time, or is always saying the wrong thing all the time. "A prudent man conceals knowledge, but the heart of fools proclaims foolishness" (Prov. 12:23). Again, notice what Proverbs says, "Wise [people] store up knowledge, but the mouth of the foolish [is] near destruction" (Prov. 10:14). Also, "The tongue of the wise uses knowledge rightly, but the mouth of fools pours forth foolishness" (Prov. 15:2). This is another way of saying they're like a barrel rolling down the hill, always making noise, but there's nothing in the barrel. "A fool has no delight in understanding, but in expressing his own heart" (Prov. 18:2). So Proverbs further explains, "A fool's mouth [is] his destruction, and his lips [are] the snare of his soul" (Prov. 18:7).

The fool seldom thinks seriously, but they laugh at serious things, and make jokes of eternal things. The fool loves his frivolity, but he deceives himself, "The folly of fools [is] deceit" (14:8). "The mouth of fools pours forth foolishness" (Prov. 15:2).

Fools will not listen to good counsel, "Because they hated knowledge and did not choose the fear of the Lord, they would have none of my counsel [and] despised my every rebuke" (Prov. 1:29, 30).

Those who try to teach fools waste their time. "He who corrects a scoffer gets shame for himself, and he who rebukes a wicked [man only] harms himself" (Prov. 9:7). That's because fools reject what you say. The opposite is also true, "Teach a just [man,] and he will increase in learning" (Prov. 9:9).

A fool is ungrateful. Gratitude is the best remembered of all virtues, and is a character trait taught by parents to children. A fool will not listen to the instructions of his parents (Prov. 15:20), and will cause them great grief (Prov. 10:1). Eventually the parents of the fool can never be proud of their foolish child.

Not only does a fool reject knowledge, a fool will deceive others to get them to believe a lie. "The wisdom of the prudent [is] to understand his way, but the folly of fools [is] deceit" (Prov. 14:8). A fool not only doesn't speak the truth, he will slander those who oppose him,

"Whoever spreads slander [is] a fool" (Prov. 10:18). And a fool usually wants to argue, "[It is] honorable for a man to stop striving, since any fool can start a quarrel" (Prov. 20:3). Not only does he start an argument, he threatens physical violence or gets others involved in fights, because "violence covers the mouth of the wicked" (Prov. 10:6).

As we describe the fool, we must be careful of Jesus' warning, "Whoever says, 'You fool!' shall be in danger of hell fire" (Matt. 5:22). We are not calling anyone a fool; we are only describing what God says of the fool. First, God calls people "fools" because they choose to ignore God and go their selfish ways (Ps. 14:1; 53:1). Second, we are usually guilty of the accusations we make of others. So if we foolishly called someone a fool, we'd be headed for the same destruction as the fool. Finally, when we put the label "fool" on anyone, they might try to fulfill our prediction, rather than repenting. They we are partly responsible for their judgment (Jas. 5:20).

Your Relationship to a Fool

1. *Don't live on the level of a fool.* The fool does his own thing and disobeys the law. Don't let the fool drag you down to his level of transgression. The fool speaks without thinking and is given to anger. When we speak without thinking, we act like a fool, and when our anger controls us, we become like them. The Proverbs tell us to never answer a fool, or else we will become like him (Prov. 26:4).

2. *Don't compliment a fool.* Fools are self-righteous; they will take any compliment as reinforcement for the stupid things they do, or the things they do the wrong way. Never give a fool any honor (Prov. 26:1). When you answer a fool, the *King James Version* says, "Lest he be wise in his own conceit [Heb. Eyes]" (Prov. 26:5). This does not mean the fool will become wise, but rather he will reinforce his own selfish opinion because you have complimented him. Then the fool will continue in his downward path to destruction. So, don't compliment them for the foolish things they do.

3. *Don't try to correct a fool.* A fool will not listen to good instruction, nor does he want to do the right thing. He will not listen to rebuke or good advice. As a matter of fact, when you correct a fool, he will rebuke you, and when you criticize a fool, he will insult you. "Do not correct a scoffer, lest he hate you; rebuke a wise [man,] and he will love you" (Prov. 9:8).

4. *Let a fool learn from the consequences of his actions.* The Bible teaches, "The way of transgressors [is] hard" (Prov. 13:15 KJV). A fool who goes his own way will eventually suffer the consequences of foolish actions. This may be judgment of sin, or just the consequences of their stupid acts, but these consequences could be instrumental in helping the fool see the folly of his way.

When the Bible says, "In the mouth of a fool [is] a rod of pride" (Prov. 14:3), it means that when a fool says foolish things, he is punished with the "rod" of consequences from what he said. This is also seen, "A fool's lips enter into contention, and his mouth calls for blows" (Prov. 18:6), telling us that a foolish man is punished because he opens his mouth to say stupid things.

Again the Scriptures teach, "Luxury is not fitting for a fool" (Prov. 19:10). Not that a fool shouldn't have good things, nor should they have luxury, but when a fool is given riches, he will squander them. When a fool is given money, he will lose it; when a fool is provided with luxurious living, he is not smart enough to keep it. In today's language, give a fool a penthouse and he'll trash it, or, give a fool a new Cadillac and he can't keep it running.

5. *Fools cannot be reasoned with so let them learn from their mistakes.* The book of Proverbs states that a fool cannot be reasoned with, nor can he learn from wise counsel. It seems mistakes are the only effective method from which they learn, especially when they suffer painful consequences. "A whip for the horse, a bridle for the donkey, and a rod for the fool's back" (Prov. 26:3). This does not mean a fool should be whipped because he is stupid. The picture here is of one who refuses to obey traffic laws, and has to pay a fine or go to jail. Isn't it foolish to lose your freedom because you won't obey the law? So a whip can teach a horse how to obey, and a bridle can teach a donkey to follow commands, but only punishment can help a fool. "When the scoffer is punished, the simple is made wise" (Prov. 21:11).

Do not get the wrong impression about fools, the book of Proverbs is not teaching that they should be punished because they are incapable of learning. No! They suffer consequences because they refuse to learn. And the person who refuses to learn from his mistakes is more foolish than the one who makes mistakes. Proverbs give us a picture of a fool being ground up because he will not learn, "Though you grind a fool in a mortar with a pestle along with crushed grain, [yet] his foolishness will not depart from him" (Prov. 27:22).

29

The basic lesson of Proverbs is: don't treat the scab, but rather get down to the infection that causes the wound. Don't treat the foolish symptoms of the fool, but rather apply medicine to the cause of the problem. The problem of the fool is that he has chosen to reject God and reject truth. He is stupid because he chooses to do stupid things. The answer of the book of Proverbs is wisdom, "How long, you simple ones, will you love simplicity? . . . and fools hate knowledge. Turn at my rebuke; surely I will pour out my spirit on you; I will make my words known to you" (Prov. 1:22-23). Proverbs indicate a fool can become wise if he will cease trusting in himself and trust in God. A fool could become wise if he would cease following his own way and follow the way of God.

6. *You should not fellowship with fools.* Proverbs tell us, "Go from the presence of a foolish man, when you do not perceive [in him] the lips of knowledge" (Prov. 14:7). Why is that? Because foolishness is infectious, those hanging around a foolish person become foolish with them. Why? Because everyone has a selfish nature, and the fool who is addicted to his selfish nature gets those around him to give into their selfish nature. Therefore, those around the fool become lazy, liars, corrupt, and blinded by their own pathetic rationalization, just like the fool.

A fool can hurt you. Proverbs say, "Let a man meet a bear robbed of her cubs, Rather than a fool in his folly" (Prov. 17:12). Foolish people never build up those around them. Rather, by sarcasm and cruel accusations, they drag everyone down to their level. Also, when you become a friend to a fool, he will feed off you and sap the life out of you. Like a mother bear that will tear you limb to limb for stealing her cubs, so a fool will leave you maimed and wounded.

Also, observe the opposite. While the folly of a fool is infectious, the wisdom of a wise man usually is not. Just hanging around wise people doesn't make you wise. To be wise, you must listen to the "right thoughts" of the wise person and attempt to do "wise things."

7. *You should do everything possible to get away from a fool.* Because a fool will harm you, don't stay anywhere around them. "Cast out the scoffer and contention will leave" (Prov. 22:10).

This is in keeping with New Testament teaching that Christians should not fellowship with unsaved people or listen to them and become like them. Paul writes, "And what accord has Christ with Belial? Or what part has a believer with an unbeliever? And what agreement has the temple of God with idols? For you are the temple of the living God. As God has said: 'I will dwell in them and walk among [them.] I will be their God, and they shall be My people'" (2 Cor. 6:15,16). So, the church was instructed to put away those who were unruly and caused contention with its ranks (Matt. 18:15-17).

Conclusion

Whether you're a Christian or not, the principles contained in Proverbs will help you live a better life. When you do right, you lay the foundation for becoming righteous before God. Your good works of righteousness will not qualify you to stand before God. But look at it in the opposite light. Those who want to believe right and do right will have a foundation to accept the Bible teaching how to obtain righteousness. To do right, they will accept the righteousness of Jesus Christ (Rom. 5:1) and be saved by faith.

CHAPTER 2
Good Decisions Will Treat You Right

Lord, I receive Your Word as
A child receives instruction from a parent.
I hide Your instructions
Deep within my heart.
I will open my ears
To hear and understand Your wisdom.
I will passionately seek to know You
And tell others what I understand.
I want Your knowledge more than money
And more than a hidden pot of gold.

Lord, teach me to reverence Your ways
And know how You want me to live.
So give me wisdom to know You
And obey what You tell me to do.

Lord, I know there is abundant wisdom
For those who seek to live the right way;
And You protect those who know You,
Who attempt to walk the right way.
You show the right paths
To those who make right decisions.

Lord, when I honestly seek to do the right thing,
Your Spirit helps me know what to do,
And He guides me in good paths.

When I experience Your wisdom,
I direct my life correctly;
And I enjoy fellowship with You.

When I experience Your wisdom,
I don't make bad decisions
And I don't make mistakes.
Then evil people don't take advantage of me
Nor do they talk me into bad decisions.
Evil people reject Your ways of thinking
And refuse to live by Your principles.
Evil people also love to think evil and do evil
And brag about it to everyone.

Lord, deliver me from a flirtatious woman
Who tries to flatter me with her words.
She had rejected the right way about sex
And turned her back on Your rules of purity.
A man is heading toward a disastrous death
When he has sex with her.
No one who goes to bed with her
Can be blameless in their own eyes;
They are headed toward Hell.

But when I obey Your wisdom, O Lord,
I am headed toward eternal life.
I am on the right path,
Because those who follow Your principles
Will enter into fellowship with You
And stay there as long as they obey You.
But the rebellious will eventually die
And not enjoy fellowship with You.
Amen

Proverbs

CHAPTER 3
Learning from Correction

Lord, I will not forget Your principles,
But I will live the way You direct.
I know that Your principles
Will give me satisfaction
And help me live a long time.
Don't let Your mercy and truth forsake me;
I will post your laws where I will constantly see them
And will meditate on them continually.
I know when Your principles control my thought processes,
You'll add value to my life
And others will respect my commitment to truth.

Lord, I will trust in You
With all my heart.
I will not lean on the old way of doing things
Nor will I make decisions apart from You.
In all my actions
I will acknowledge You
And You will direct my paths.
I will not do things my own way
Nor prize my opinions over Yours.
I will reverence You in all I do
And separate myself from all appearances of evil.
Your paths shall make me wise and healthy;
Your ways shall make me strong.

Lord, I give you all that I have;
I will bring a tithe of everything to You.
You promise that my checking account will have enough,
You will meet all my needs as they come.

Lord, I will not complain when You punish me
Because I know You correct wrong actions.
I know You're my heavenly Father
Who loves and cares for me.
And You correct me when I disobey,
Just as an earthly father corrects his child.
I'll rejoice when I find Your principles
And know how to direct my life.
Your correction is a valuable gift,
Better than a gift of money.
Your correction is better than expensive jewelry;
Nothing can compare to Your care of me.
When I do the things You teach me,
I'll live longer than those who reject Your way.
And I'll be more satisfied than a rich person;
I'll be more honored than a famous person.
And I'll have a pleasant life;
I'll live in peace.
Your principles can give everyone a good life;
Everyone can enjoy Your happiness.

Lord, You created natural laws to rule the earth,
Your principles guide the universe.
You had a reason for creating the seas,
And You directed rain to fall on the earth.
Since You have the power and wisdom to create all things,
I won't neglect Your laws for me;
I will live by Your principles.

Lord, I know Your laws will enrich my life;
They help me do all I should do.

Your principles guide my daily life;
They keep me from making terrible mistakes.
When I lie down to go to sleep at night,
My conscience won't keep me awake.
And I will trust You when the wicked come,
Bringing sudden terror and destruction.
Because I have yielded to Your paths,
You will not let anything happen to me
That is not within Your plan.

Lord, I will not withhold good from anyone
Who is entitled to it,
When I am able to give it.
I will not tell the needy to go away
And come back tomorrow,
If I can give them help immediately.
I will not plan to hurt my neighbor
Who lives peaceably with me.
I will not fuss needlessly with anyone
When there is no reason to disagree.
I will not look up to oppressive people
Nor follow their example,
Because I know they are an abomination to You
And You have cursed them.

Lord, You have told me inwardly how to live
And You bless the home of those who live right.
I know You scorn the scorner
And You give grace to the humble.
You give honor to those who honor You
While You neglect those who neglect You.
Amen

CHAPTER 4
Listening To Parents' Advice

Lord, I will listen to the instructions of my father
In order to gain understanding,
Because I know I have a good life
When I don't go against his advice.
My father was once a child to his father,
And my mother loved me tenderly.
He wanted me to respect his advice
So I could have a happy and prosperous life.
My father told me to acquire as much education
As I could master,
And not go against the things I learned.
He told me to guard the way I think
And it would guard my life.

Lord, the first thing I want to get is wisdom
And make sure I apply it to my life.
When I make understanding first in my life,
It will make me first in the life of others.
My understanding will make me honorable
When I honor the pursuit of wisdom.

Lord, I will learn wisdom from my father
So I will live a long life.
My father endeavored to teach me the right things
So I could live the right way.

Then when I walk, my steps won't stumble;
And when I run, I'll not fall down.

I'll learn from my father's discipline
And not forget how he directed me,
For it is the essence of my life-purpose.

Lord, I'll not follow wicked people,
Nor will I do things evil people do.
I'll avoid what they do
And go the opposite way;
For they can't rest well,
Unless they have rebelled against the law
And caused others to do the same thing.
Their whole passion is doing their own thing
And causing others to rebel against Your ways.

Lord, I know the path of people who do right
Gets brighter every day,
And leads toward the shining light.
But the path of those who do wicked things
Gets darker all the time,
And eventually they stumble in their night.

Lord, I will pay attention to what my father says
And listen to his wise advice.
I will not turn away from his counsel
Nor will I refuse to listen to his direction,
Because his instructions will make things easier
And enrich all I do in life.

Lord, I will focus my heart on You
And do everything my father says.
I will not turn my back on him,
Nor will I refuse to obey him,

Because those who listen will prosper outwardly
And get great satisfaction inwardly.

Lord, above everything else I do,
I will guard my heart

For it directs all I do in life.
I'll always tell the truth
According to what I know in my heart.
I'll always follow the right paths
According to where my heart directs me.
I'll not turn to the left or right
And I'll always turn away from evil.
Amen

CHAPTER 5
Beware of the Trollop

Lord, help me listen to wise advice
And understand helpful counsel,
That I may learn life-improving principles,
And not forget beneficial truth.

Lord, I know a tempting woman tells lies,
Sweet little tales to get her way,
Slithering words make her happy.
She will make my life bitter.
Her mouth will cut me up and down,
Her feet will lead to my death;
She will guide me straight to Hell.
I will go the opposite way and seek the path of life,
The woman's path is slippery;
No one knows where she leads.

Lord, You said to listen to You
And to follow Your direction.
You said get away from that woman
And stay away from her house,
Lest I sacrifice my good honor
And destroy my faithful years.
Then, will I grieve in old age
Because my lust consumed my life.

Lord, the man who chases skirts hates Your advice
And despises Your reproof of his sin.
He refuses to listen to those who point out his stupidity
And turns his back on those who warn him.

Lord, evil almost got me
And I was a good church member.
I realize I must drink from my own well
And not sacrifice my life to the lust of the flesh.
I must preserve my own self-esteem
And not give it away.
Then You will bless my decisions
And I will rejoice with my spouse.
She shall give me comfort and strength
And I will be happy with her,
And we will be happy with each other.

Lord, I will not be ravished with a whorish woman
Nor find my love with a trollop.
Every one of my actions are always seen by You
And You know everything I do.
Those who sin against You,
Shall be a prisoner to their iniquity;
Their lust shall become their punishment.
They shall die without knowing anything better;
And the greatest consequence of their sin,
Is that it drives them away from You.
Amen

CHARACTER SKETCH:

The Trollop

The loose woman described in Proverbs is a trollop, which *Webster* defines as, "A slovenly, dirty woman, a sexually promiscuous woman, a prostitute."[1] The *Oxford English Dictionary* adds, "An untidy, or slovenly woman, a slattern."[2] The word *trollop* comes from *troll*, which originally meant to sing in a full, rolling voice. However, the second meaning was to fish with a moving line, working up and down, or trailing behind a boat. A troll is a lure used to catch fish. And doesn't that describe a trollop? A woman who is moving around like a fishing line being constantly cast into the water to lure or catch fish. But the trollop is not catching fish, she's catching men. Other synonyms for trollop are slut, hussy, adulteress, and fornicator. American high school girls call a girl a *ho* when she acts like a trollop.

A trollop never thinks about her own spiritual condition, nor the fate of what will happen to her body or soul (Prov. 5:6, 9:13). Nor does she tell the men that she seduces that they are being led inevitably to destruction (Prov. 2:18,19; 6:26; 7:22,23; 9:18).

A trollop dresses seductively (Prov. 7:10) and entices men with her outward beauty (Prov. 2:16,17). Proverbs warn, "Do not lust after her beauty in your heart" (Prov. 6:25) for it is only adorned with outward makeup, suggestive clothing, and perfume.

The New Testament suggests there are three things that tempt a man to sin, "For all that [is] in the world—the lust of the flesh, the lust of the eyes, and the pride of life—is not of the Father but is of the world" (1 John 2:16). So the trollop uses all three to tempt a man. First, she knows a man wants to satisfy his physical sexual appetite, so she offers him sex. No one really knows why an adulteress tempts a man with sex, but she knows that it works. Second, the trollop uses the lust of the eyes to tempt a man, so she casts her beauty and flashing eyes as a lure to tempt a man into a sexual tryst. In the third place, the trollop appeals to the pride of life, a man's ego. The trollop entices a man by flattering him. The trollop knows the male wants to dominate, to be "Number One," and the whorish woman provides that thrill. A man's ego is independently rebellious to any control, so the trollop tempts him to stray from the path of God (Prov. 2:16,17), come to her bed (Prov. 7:16), and enjoy the experience of "prohibitive dreams" (Prov. 7:18). But what the man doesn't know is that when he thinks he is "Number One," the trollop has really won, and he is in her bondage.

The trollop offers everything the man thinks he really wants. The male ego likes to be flattered, and anyone simple enough to give into her flattery will be destroyed. The trollop catches and kisses the simple man (Prov. 7:13) then tells him their sexual escapade is safe, "[I have] peace offerings with me; today I have paid my vows" (Prov. 7:14). She also promises that they will be uninterrupted, "For my husband [is] not at home; he has gone on a long journey" (Prov. 7:19).

The writer uses Proverbs to warn against the trollop, "Can a man take fire to his bosom, and his clothes not be burned?" (Prov. 6:27). In return, the trollop uses a Proverb to entice a man, "Stolen water is sweet, And bread [eaten] in secret is pleasant" (Prov. 9:17). She is suggesting that stolen water—sex outside of marriage—is sweeter than drinking "from your own well" (Prov. 5:15). The trollop offers momentary pleasure that is short lived, while her sex has long-range venomizing consequences.

The godly woman is the opposite of the trollop. "Charm [is] deceitful and beauty [is] passing, but a woman [who] fears the Lord, she shall be praised" (Prov. 31:30).

How the Trollop Tempts

1. Flattery (Prov. 2:16; 6:24; 7:5; 21:2).
2. Sweet talk (Prov. 5:3).

3. Outward beauty (Prov. 6:25).
4. Flirts with the eyes (Prov. 6:25).
5. On the prowl, looking for the naïve man (Prov. 6:26; 7:13).
6. Sexually revealing dress (Prov. 7:10).
7. Restless with her life (Prov. 7:11,12).
8. Offers a place for sex (Prov. 7:12,13).
9. Sex is spoken of openly, yet discreetly (Prov. 7:16-18).
10. Her object is sex (Prov. 6:32).

The Book of Proverbs tells a young man that a trollop is the wrong type of companionship. She will not give the man love, companionship, nor will she make him a good wife. She cannot be trusted because if she will cheat on her present husband, she'll cheat on the next one. Proverbs teaches that a young man should seek a virtuous wife (Prov. 31:10-31), and that he should choose a godly woman, while rejecting the trollop. Why? A woman's companionship offers the consequences of life or destruction.

Results of Visiting the Trollop

1. The wrath of a betrayed husband (Prov. 6:34,35).
2. Loss of finances (Prov. 6:31).
3. Guilt (Prov. 6:29).
4. Physical destruction (Prov. 7:22).
5. Spiritual destruction (Prov. 7:27).

Proverbs have described it correctly, i.e., the balance of power between the sexes. It's the woman who knows a man, knows what he wants, and knows how to use her body for sexual favors. It's the woman who gets what she wants from a man. While it appears that the woman is the one being deceived, in a bottom-line analysis; the woman is more in control of the situation than the man.

And what about the male? He is so driven by his sexual appetite that he is blind to what a woman is capable of. She doesn't necessarily want sex, she uses it to get control over the man. He seldom understands the total circumstances of the tryst. The bottom line: men don't completely understand women, but women understand men. As a result, men are usually gullible pawns when they fall into the clutches of a trollop.

ENDNOTES

1. *Webster's, New World Dictionary of the American Language, 2nd College Ed.* (Cleveland, OH: William Collins/World Publishing Co., Inc., 1974).

2. Answers.com http://www.answers.com/trollop, accessed 14 February 2005.

Proverbs

CHAPTER 6

Work Hard and Watch Out for Loose Women

Lord, I will not co-sign a friend's loan,
Nor will I shake hands on a bad deal,
Because my agreement will become a trap
And my words will come back to haunt me.
I will get out of every bad arrangement,
Then I won't lose my friends
When they try to take advantage of me.

Lord, I will be responsible for my livelihood,
I won't sleep when I should work.
I won't get caught in a bad deal
When the swindler tries to trap me.
I will learn from the industrious ants
Who have learned to work diligently,
Even when no one makes them work.
They work continually in the summer,
So they'll have food after the harvest is over.
I will not be a lazy sluggard,
But will awaken to do my responsibilities.
The sluggard closes his eyes to his job,
He folds his hands instead of working.
He shall be poor because of his procrastination,
As though a thief has stolen everything he possessed.

Lord, I will not be a wicked man
Who makes promises he doesn't plan to keep,
Who winks his eye at evil,
Yet sins with his hands and feet.
I will not plan evil to get ahead,
Nor will I entertain myself with sin.
I know the evil man will be judged suddenly;
His punishment will break him in two.

Lord, I know You hate six things,
And the seventh is an abomination to You.
First, is an arrogant attitude
And second, a lying tongue.
Third, You hate hands that shed innocent blood,
And fourth, a heart that thinks evil.
The fifth, are feet that lead to trouble,
And sixth, is a false witness who lies.
The seventh is the worst of all:
The gossip who continually stirs up trouble among brethren.

Lord, I will keep my father's rules,
And will not displease my mother.
I will memorize them carefully
And repeat them daily as I try to live right.
I want them to lead me to success,
And keep me when I sleep
And refresh me when I awake.

Lord, Your commandments are a light to my feet
And light to my path.
Your commandments correct me when I stray,
And will renew my life.

Lord, let Your commandments keep me from a trollop,
Who will flatter to seduce me.
I will not lust after her beauty,

Nor will her fluttering eyelids tempt me.
A man will not be worth two cents
Who falls to the temptation of a whorish woman
Because the adulteress woman will snare his life.
Can I put fire inside my shirt
Without burning my clothes?
Can I walk on flaming hot coals
Without burning my feet?
Neither can I have sex with another woman
Without searing my conscience and reputation.

Lord, people do not hate a thief who steals because he is hungry.
But when a thief is caught,
He must repay sevenfold for his crime.
He who has sex outside his marriage
Must pay restitution like the thief,
He may have to sacrifice all the wealth he has accumulated.
He who commits adultery is a fool;
He destroys himself.
He will get nothing but punishment and embarrassment
And he will never forget his escapade.
Because jealousy boils over into rage,
The offended man will not show mercy
When he takes revenge.
He will not accept your apology,
Nor any other way you try to appease him.
Amen

Proverbs

CHAPTER 7
A Description of One Who Despises Wisdom

Lord, I will obey the directions of my father
And not forget what he expects of me.
I will obey the commandments in every area of life
And will not shut my eyes to any directive.
Like a string tied on my finger,
My heart will never forget them;
And wisdom will talk to me like an older sister,
So I will please my whole family.

Lord, Your wisdom will keep me from the seductive trollop
Who will tempt me with her flattery.
I was looking out my window of my home
And saw a naïve youth who lacked common sense.
He was hanging around a dressed-up trollop
And was stupid enough to keep talking to her;
He wasn't wise enough to flee danger.
He accepted her invitation to go to her place.
It was dark so he thought no one would see him;
But evening twilight always turns dark,
And he was blinded by the blackness of evil.

The woman was dressed in sexually revealing clothes,
But she was not beautiful;
Rather, she was a "ho," just cheap trailer trash.
She did not value her home or reputation
But prowled the bars to pick up men.

She flirted with the naive youth
And blew him a kiss, then winked at him.
"We're made for each other," she coaxed him;
Then she said, "Where have you been all my life?"
"I've been looking for someone like you," she continued,
"Now I'm not going to let you get away!"
"You'll love my apartment," as she invited him to her place;
"It's where a man can really feel happy."
"Let's spend the night together," she tempted him,
"We'll experience more exciting love
Than we've had with anyone else."
She told the gullible youth, "My man is gone
And won't return until next week."
"He's got a lot to do in another town,
And no one will ever know."

Because the trollop knows the weaknesses of men,
The naïve youth helplessly gives in to her offer.
He follows her like a fatted animal to its slaughter
Or like a convicted felon to the electric chair.
He takes a bullet in his gut,
And like a fish swallowing a lure,
He never realized she leads to death.

Lord, I will seek out wise advice
And do exactly as I am told.
I will not reject good counsel,
Nor will I turn my back on godly advisors.
I know the trollop has wounded many gullible men;
She's even destroyed strong men.
Her bed is not Heaven, but Hell;
It leads straight to death.
Amen

Proverbs

CHAPTER **8**
A Defense of Right-Believing

Lord, You were eternally wise
Long before You created the earth.
You made everything by Your principles
Long before there were ocean depths
And before there were artesian springs.
You did everything by the laws of Your wisdom
Before mountains were put in their place,
Before hills were created.
You followed the right way of doing things
When You established Heaven as Your sanctuary
And determined the constant direction of the compass.
You were guided by eternal laws
When You created the clouds;
From them comes the rain upon the earth.
You established the boundary of Your creation;
The seas will not cover the dry land,
And the earth will be controlled by the laws You established.

Lord, You bless those who now live by Your wisdom
And attempt to live in harmony with Your laws.
You want everyone to seek Your principles
And not refuse the wisdom that comes from You.
Those who attempt to learn Your laws
Are attempting to live by Your standards,
For they will get Your favor
And will have a better life.

But those who reject Your requirements,
Sin against themselves
And eventually will suffer the consequences of broken laws.

Lord, I take the wisdom You offer to all;
Your wise advice is good for me.
Like a salesman who sells his merchandise,
You have offered me many ways to become wise.
I can become a better manager of my life
When I direct my life by principles,
And I can become a better family member.
Anyone can be smarter than they are;
Anyone can have a better life.
The naïve can be successful if he'll get wisdom,
And the loser can learn from his mistakes.

Lord, You offer me a better life by following good principles;
You offer me the ability to make right decisions.
Help me to say the right things
And not act foolish and sound stupid.
Help my advice to be practical and morally right,
So those who listen to me will succeed.
Those who are smart will recognize my wisdom;
Those who are moral will value my principles.

Lord, I know the wages of wisdom are better than silver
And those who continually learn the right things
Will receive more than gold.
Wisdom is more valuable than the finest jewels;
Nothing can be compared to a knowing mind.
Wisdom will always lead me to do the appropriate thing
And will help me solve problems and be creative.

Lord, I reject pride, stepping on people, and breaking the law;
I will always put You first in my life.
I will follow right principles in mapping out my life

So I will have a basis to make good choices.
I will follow time-proven management principles
Because managers-in-training must follow them.
Wisdom loves those who follow its principles
And I will love wisdom to become smarter.
Wise people will become richer and get more honor,
Because they have something greater than earthly treasure;
They will receive more than tangible goods,
And more than wages, stock options, or retirement benefits.
They develop godly inner character;
Their inner peace and happiness will be priceless.
Amen

Proverbs

CHAPTER 9
Foolish-Believing Leads to Destruction

Lord, I know that everything worthwhile in life
Is built on Your wise principles.
Those who live wisely have plenty of meat to eat,
And plenty to drink,
And a table full of delicious desserts.
Those who live wisely give good advice to others;
They freely share what they have learned.
Those who are gullible should learn from their wisdom,
So should those who want to improve themselves.
They should desire to learn as much as they hunger for a meal,
And seek wisdom as much as they thirst for water.
Those who are foolish should repent of their stubborn ways
And embrace Your wisdom.

Lord, I know when I reprove scorners,
They will hate my advice.
When I instruct a wise man,
I know he will listen to what I tell him
Because the wise man wants to learn from others
So he can improve himself, his family and his business.

Lord, it is smart to put You at the center of my life
And I'll become holy as I follow Your principles.
When I live smart, I'll live longer;
And I'll enjoy the days You give me.

For Your wisdom will make me a better person,
While the negative person makes his life more bitter.

Lord, I know a woman is foolish when she's a busybody;
The more she thinks she learns from gossip,
The dumber she becomes.
She always runs to hear more gossip,
Yet she is both foolish and uneducated;
Only naïve people listen to her.
She delights to hear about those who are having an affair
Because she thinks stolen waters are sweet,
And bread eaten in secret is pleasurable.
She doesn't realize she's enjoying gossiping
About those who rebel against God,
And about those going to Hell.
Amen

 *Proverbs*

CHAPTER **10**
Right-Believing Leads to Success

Lord, I know wise sons please their fathers,
But a foolish son weighs heavily on his mother.
All the wealth of wickedness can't give inner happiness,
But those who live right have peace the world can't enjoy.

Lord, I know You give a full life to those who live right,
But the rebel will never find happiness.
The lazy man will eventually be poor,
But the diligent will become prosperous.
Smart young men work hard in the growing season,
But foolish young men play during the harvest.

Lord, You add value to those who live by right principles,
But those who rebel against Your laws
Suffer the consequences of their broken laws.
I like to remember those who do their duty,
But the memory of the rebel stinks.
Those who are wise will try to do Your commandments,
But a bragging fool will fail to do right.
Those who live uprightly will have confidence,
But those who undermine the steps of others
Will eventually fail at all they do.
Those who overlook the sin of others and their mistakes
Will eventually suffer for their oversight.
Those who speak the right things will help others;
And those who condone breaking Your principles

Will eventually suffer the violence of those broken laws.
Those who love, overlook the faults of others;
But those who hate, stir up strife.

Lord, I find wise thinking in wise men;
But the fool that rejects good advice
Deserves the punishment he receives.
Wise men want to learn more wise things,
But fools don't care about learning anything;
They are destroying any chance of a good life.
A wise man has many kinds of treasures,
They protect him in many ways;
But the fool has only his poverty
Which cannot protect him from destruction.
The life-work of those who do right
Gives them the life they want to live.
The sin of a fool is simply doing nothing,
And the laziness of a fool gives him nothing.

Lord, those who follow Your unchangeable principles
Are walking in the way of eternal life.
A fool lies to hide his hatred
And slanders those who oppose his way of life.
The wise are able to discipline their words;
The more some people try to explain away their failure,
The more I know they are lying.
The works of people who do right are worth lots of money,
But the heart of an evil man is not worth much.
The speech of people who do right helps many,
But people die who listen to the words of a fool.

Lord, Your blessings make me rich
And You don't add sorrow to it.
The fool has fun breaking Your laws,
But those who give themselves to wisdom know better.
The wicked usually experience the thing they fear,

And those who desire to do right
Usually get what they want in life.
The death of the wicked comes like a blowing wind,
They are gone and nothing remains.
Those who do right also die,
But they leave a lasting influence in other people.
Those who are lazy sluggards
Are like a vile taste to the tongue,
Like smoke that irritates the eyes.

Lord, You lengthen the years of those who do right,
But shorten the life of the wicked.
The dreams of those who do right bring joy,
But the expectations of the wicked pass away.

Lord, doing Your will gives me strength,
But the strength of those who rebel against You will be dissipated.
Those who do right will speak right things,
But the tongue of the wicked is worthless.
Those who do right will know what to say,
But those who do evil never have the right words.
Those who do right will live forever,
But those who do wickedness will not inhabit the earth.
Amen

CHARACTER SKETCH:

The Wicked

"The wicked man does deceptive work" (Prov. 11:18). "But in the revenue of the wicked is trouble" (Prov. 15:6). "The righteous is delivered from trouble, and it comes to the wicked instead" (Prov. 11:8). "The wicked is ensnared by the transgression of his lips" (Prov. 12:13). "Though they join forces, the wicked will not go unpunished" (Prov. 11:21). "The thoughts of the wicked are an abomination to the Lord" (Prov. 15:26).

The Book of Proverbs observes that the wicked seem to eventually fail. While some wicked people may enjoy temporary success, their joy or prosperity is not permanent. The person who lives right should not envy the evil man, nor should he follow his example. "Do not fret because of evildoers; don't envy the wicked. For the evil have no future; their light will be snuffed out" (Prov. 24:19, 20 NLT).

The evil man earns money by deception. That means they do not give an honest day's work for an honest day's pay; they deceive their employer. It also means they are not honest with money, and will not give an accurate account of finances entrusted to them. When they sell you something, it is not as they claim, and when they tell you they will do something, they don't keep their promise.

The wicked has trouble with his income. Sometimes the wicked will earn a lot of money deceitfully; at other times they will try to keep it deceitfully. "But in the revenue of the wicked is trouble" (Prov. 15:6). That means they don't get to enjoy the money they earn deceptively, usually their money brings them trouble.

Trouble chases the wicked man. Even though the wicked person seems to have a good life, trouble usually catches up to him. Why is that? Because when he breaks the rules, he walks so close to the edge that occasionally he trips over the rules. What happens to a person who is tripped up? They're embarrassed and usually they hurt themselves. Sometimes they hurt others, and many lose their way in life.

"Evil pursues sinners" (Prov. 13:21). Proverbs gives us this picture of evil chasing the wicked man; but in reality, it's the other way around. The wicked man chases evil until he catches the punishment associated with evil.

Those who live by right principles are usually delivered from trouble, "The righteous is delivered from trouble, and it comes to the wicked instead" (Prov. 11:8). This means that trouble doesn't usually catch the righteous man, but turns on the wicked man. "There shall no evil happen to the just: but the wicked shall be filled with mischief" (Prov. 12:21 KJV).

The wicked man is caught in the trap he lays for others. But the unfaithful will be caught by their lust (Prov. 11:6). That means when a liar tells lies about someone at work, it usually comes back to hurt the liar. And when the thief steals from someone, he usually loses his ill-gain to another thief. "The wicked is ensnared by the transgression of his lips" (Prov. 12:13).

The wicked rarely accomplishes his hopes and dreams. In a world run by laws, those who break laws, seldom accomplish what they want in life. When the wicked tries to horde the money he got dishonestly, "The Lord . . . casts away the desire of the wicked" (Prov. 10:3). He will not get what he wants, "The expectation of the wicked will perish" (Prov. 10:28). The wicked shall not get the happiness he wants, but usually gets the opposite, "But the expectation of the wicked is wrath" (Prov. 11:23).

God is against the wicked. "The way of the wicked is an abomination to the Lord" (Prov. 15:9). God will not let him get away with his rebellion, and even when the consequences of his actions do not immediately punish him, God has judgment reserved for the wicked. "Though they join forces, the wicked will not go unpunished" (Prov. 11:21). God will condemn a man of wicked intentions (Prov. 12:2). God not only rejects the rebellion of the wicked, God hates his thoughts of rebellion and his evil plans of sin. "The thoughts of the wicked are an abomination to the Lord" (Prov. 15:26).

Conclusion

Proverbs describes punishment on the wicked. While they seem to get rich off their wicked acts, they do not get the happiness they work for. Eventually, they lose their fortune. Every person has a sinful nature, and it seems so easy to follow the path of evil. But Proverbs says there is no happiness to evil people, but eventually they will be punished by the evil consequences of the things they do.

 *Proverbs*

CHAPTER 11

Wrong-Believing Leads to Failure

Lord, I know You hate false advertisements,
But delight when I tell the truth.
When I follow Your principles, I have true self-understanding;
But those driven by ego end up embarrassing themselves.

Lord, I want to be guided by integrity,
Because the lies of rebels shall destroy them.

Lord, I want Your deliverance when I live right,
Because money will not help when You judge the wicked.
You deliver me when I live right,
But the dreams of rebels will never happen,
And the plans of the law-breakers perish with them.

Lord, You deliver me when I know the truth,
But the lies of a hypocrite destroy his neighbor.
The city rejoices when its inhabitants do right,
And they shout when rebels are punished.
The city is blessed when it obeys Your laws,
But is overthrown when it listens to the evil speech of the rebels.

Lord, I will not tell everything I know;
But those who hate their neighbor are not smart.
They spread the dirt of gossip about them.

Lord, I know faithful friends don't embarrass others.
Those who seek wisdom get safe advice,
But those who listen to fools will be tripped up.
I know I'll end up paying what is owed
If I sign a note for someone I don't know.

Lord, a gracious woman is loved,
But hateful people are hated by others.
A strong man is respected,
And a merciful man gets mercy.
Those who plant a good seed will get a good harvest,
But a wicked man sows deceit.

Lord, I know those who do right get life,
But those who run after evil end up with death.

Lord, those who do right are Your delight,
But those who lie are an abomination to You.
Those who do right plant good seeds,
And one wicked person can't keep another from being punished.
A beautiful woman who acts like a fool
Is like a beautiful jewel in a pig's nose.

Lord, those who do right dream of being good,
But the rebel can only expect wrath.
Those who give away goods, eventually get them back,
And those who withhold their goods end up in poverty.

Lord, You bless the generous soul;
And those who add value to others will have value added to them.
People bless those who provide it for them,
But curse those who will not sell them food.
Those who diligently seek good will find it,
And those who seek evil will be found by it;
Because what goes around, comes back around.
Those who believe their money will get them ahead

Will always fall behind.
Those who always do the right thing
Will flourish like a fruitful farm.
Those who make trouble for their family
Will inherit a whirlwind.
And the fool will always be a slave
To the wise who do the right thing.
The fruit of those who do the right thing
Grows on the tree of the wise.
Those who do right will be rewarded with right things,
And the wicked shall be rewarded with wickedness.
Amen

CHARACTER SKETCH:

The Mischievous Person

"He who plots to do evil will be called a schemer" (Prov. 24:8). "The thoughts of the righteous [are] right, [but] the counsels of the wicked [are] deceitful" and "Deceit is in the heart of those who devise evil, but counselors of peace have joy" (Prov. 12:5,20). "He winks his eye to devise perverse things; He purses his lips [and] brings about evil" (Prov. 16:30). "A man who isolates himself seeks his own desire; He rages against all wise judgment" (Prov. 18:1).

The King James Version speaks of the mischievous person as though he is one who is up to "tricks" or making fun of people. However, the *New American Standard* Bible translates this person as a "schemer" when actually the Hebrew text means, "plotter of schemes" or "maker of plans." Clearly, the mischievous person is one who plans evil thoughts or deeds, "He who plots to do evil will be called a schemer" (Prov. 24:8). This person is described as one who "devises evil" (Prov. 12:20). The word *devise* in the Hebrew is a word for plying.

The mischievous man doesn't just pull practical jokes. He has no use for "right principles." As a result, he is often likened as unto a fool because he wants to do his own way, and have his own self-appointed goals. It is wise not to be like the mischievous man, "Do not be envious of evil men, nor desire to be with them; for their heart devises violence, and their lips talk of troublemaking" (Prov. 24:1,2).

Proverbs

CHAPTER 12
The Contrast Between Right-Believing and Wrong-Believing

Lord, I love to learn the good principles of life;
I don't want to be stubborn like those who hate to be corrected.
I will do good things to obtain Your favor;
I won't believe evil because it leads to judgment.
I shall not be established by doing wicked things,
But I will be grounded in living right.

A woman who lives by correct acts
Is a crown to her husband.
A woman who embarrasses her husband
Is like cancer in the bones.

Lord, I will believe about doing right, and will do right;
Those who listen to wicked counsel deceive themselves.

Lord, I will do right and help other people;
I will do right and build my family on a solid rock;
Wicked people hurt other people;
The wicked always fail and their names will be forgotten.

Lord, I want to be known as one who lives by Your principles
Because those who hate and criticize are despised.
Yet even those who are hated and work for their food,

Are better then lazy people who puff themselves up
And don't have anything to eat.

Lord, I am kind to my animals, yet get my work done with them.
It's better than those who speak kind words to them,
Yet treat them cruelly.
When I plow and plant my ground,
I will have bread to eat after the harvest.
But the lazy man won't do anything,
And will not have food to eat.

Lord, I want the fruit from doing right;
I don't want to follow the schemes of deceivers.
I will walk around the trouble I see,
But an evil speaking man will be tripped up by his words.
I will be satisfied with the money I agree to work for
And I will live by the things I get from my work.

Lord, the fool believes he always does the right thing,
But they who listen to wise counsel get ahead.
Everyone knows when a fool loses his temper,
But a wise man doesn't show his anger;
He says the right words slowly and quietly.
The words of a fool pierce like a knife,
But the counsel of the wise gives health.

The lies of a fool will eventually be revealed,
But no one can correct the words of a wise man.
The fool deceives people because he continually plans evil,
But those who listen to the truth will be happy.
The wicked will continually plan to do wicked things,
But the wise will continually plan to do right.

Lord, I know You hate lips that lie,
And You love those who tell the truth.

72

The fool always talks about foolish things,
And the wise man believes what is right.

Lord, I will always work diligently,
Because it will make me successful;
And the lazy will not be successful.
I will always speak good words
Because it will make life easier and happy,
But discouraging words will make an old man out of me.

Lord, when I continually live by the right principles,
I am a testimony to my neighbors.
The lazy man tries to get everyone
To live at his level of incompetence and inactivity.
The lazy man won't take advantage of his opportunities,
But the diligent turn them into money.
Those who do right, follow the path of eternal life;
The path of the procrastinator leads to death.
Amen

CHARACTER SKETCH:

The Diligent Person

"Keep your heart with all diligence, for out of it [spring] the issues of life" (Prov. 4:23). "But the soul of the diligent shall be made rich" (Prov. 13:4). "Do you see a man [who] excels in his work? He will stand before kings" (Prov. 22:29).

Webster has three definitions of diligence. First, "care, persevering application (focus)."[3] That means the diligent person is not turned away from what he is supposed to do, but is focused on his responsibilities. The second definition is "speed, haste, the attention and care legally expected or required of a person."[4] The third application is, "to be steady, earnest and energetic in application and work."[5]

Therefore, what can you say about the diligent person? The diligent person works hard, and applies himself to do right things in the right way. "Be diligent to know the state of your flocks, [and] attend to your herds" (Prov. 27:23). What happens to those who are diligent? "He who has a slack hand becomes poor, but the hand of the diligent makes rich" (Prov. 10:4). Proverbs suggests that diligence in one's occupation leads to prosperity. Also, "The lazy [man] does not roast what he took in hunting, but diligence [is] man's precious possession" (Prov. 12:27). This action suggests the diligent person conserves things and does not squander his possessions. The diligent person not only disciplines himself, he applies discipline to everything he has.

Diligence is not a skill nor is it knowledge acquired by learning. Diligence is an attitude or outlook on life. Sometimes our attitudes are also called the values or the things we prize. Therefore, if diligence is an attitude, how does the young person acquire the attitude of diligence? This person can acquire good attitudes from good role models, and/or by constantly doing the right thing or things that give good results. A young man who works for a diligent employer will learn to give diligence to his job because his employer won't let him become lazy, or a sluggard. "Do you see a man [who] excels in his work? He will stand before kings" (Prov. 22:29).

Ultimately, the diligent person rises to the top and becomes the manager of the shift, or they may even become the president of the corporation. "The hand of the diligent will rule, but the lazy [man] will be put to forced labor" (Prov. 12:24).

Like other attitudes such as kindness and generosity, the diligent can become *more* diligent by applying himself to live the attitude to which he aspires. "Keep your heart with all diligence, for out of it [spring] the issues of life" (Prov. 4:23).

Conclusion

Diligence is an attitude of both the righteous man and the wise, i.e., those who think right—the wise—eventually will do right. A diligent man will give attention to his business and will not squander his life. He is steady, dependable, and brings energy to the things he does. As a result of being diligent, he will be promoted and become prosperous.

ENDNOTES

3. *Webster's Third New International Dictionary*, unabridged (1993), s. v. "diligence."
4. *Ibid.*
5. *Ibid.*, s. v. "diligent."

CHAPTER 13
How to Live Right

Lord, I will listen to my father's wise instruction;
But a sarcastic son won't take any advice.

Lord, I will speak good words so I will prosper;
But the rebel will eventually get violence.

Lord, I will control my speech to properly discipline my life;
But they are destroyed who don't care what they say.

Lord, I will work diligently so I will prosper;
But the lazy have nothing, even though they want everything.

Lord, I will live right and speak the truth;
But the wicked will eventually be caught in his lies.
My right believing keeps me doing the right things,
But the evil desires of the wicked always trip him up.

Lord, some people dream of riches, but have nothing;
But the poor who works diligently
Can improve his bank account.

Lord, people who live right enjoy thinking the right way;
But the wicked are tripped up by their wicked thoughts.

Lord, I can learn to live right by listening to wise people;
But proud people get everyone irritated at them.

I'll increase my bank account by diligent work,
But the arrogant will lose his money when he won't take advice.

Lord, I sometimes get discouraged
When I don't reach my goals that are too lofty;
But when I accomplish the plans I make,
My life feels complete and fulfilled.

Lord, those who despise Your Word will be destroyed;
I shall be rewarded when I live by Your principles.
Right living leads me to an abundant life,
And I shall not come into eternal punishment.
Right believing helps me focus on others,
But those who break Your law will have a hard time.

Lord, help me understand the way You think
And not be like the fool who opens himself to folly.

Lord, help me be a faithful witness to my friends
And not like the wicked who deceive others.
I will learn from the admonishment of the wise,
But those who reject correction
Will be embarrassed by their failure and poverty.

Lord, I'm happy when I reach my goals in life;
But fools are never happy in their sin.

Lord, I'll make friends with people who believe right,
So they'll influence me to live right.
Those whose friends are fools,
Will suffer the same consequences as fools.
Those who live right will be rewarded by righteousness;
But evil will chase down a rebel and beat him to death.
A good man's inheritance will extend to his grandchildren,
But the inheritance of evil men will go to those who live right.

The right-living poor have enough to eat,
But wrong-believing people eventually lose everything.

Lord, I will correct my children so their decision-making
won't be corrupted,
And I demonstrate my love to them by making them do right.

Those who live right have satisfying lives,
But the desires of evil are never satisfied.
Amen

Character Sketch:

The Prudent Person

"Every prudent [man] acts with knowledge" (Prov. 13:16).
"The wisdom of the prudent [is] to understand his way"
(Prov. 14:8).

The Book of Proverbs uses the word prudence differently than we do in our current society. Today we may call a prude "a person who is excessively or priggishly attentive to propriety or decorum."[6] Also *Webster* defines a woman as a prude who shows extreme modesty.[7] However, the *Oxford Dictionary* gives a definition that says, "The ability to discern the most suitable, politic, or profitable cause of action."[8] This is the definition that best describes the prudent person in Proverbs.

Proverbs defines wisdom as right thinking which leads to right living. The wise person is also prudent, "I, wisdom, dwell with prudence" (Prov. 8:12). This means the prudish person not only is wise to know right thinking, the wise person can also discipline himself for right living. Isn't this what Proverbs says? "Every prudent [man] acts with knowledge" (Prov. 13:16).

It's important for wise people to not only study themselves to understand how they live, but to improve themselves by learning. "The wisdom of the prudent [is] to understand his way" (Prov. 14:8).

Earlier the simpleton was described as being gullible or naïve, while the wise or prudent understands how to live. "The simple believes every word, but the prudent considers well his steps" (Prov. 14:15).

The Book of Proverbs says much about learning from the consequences of life. Why? So you won't commit the same foolish mistake, over and over. "A fool despises his father's instruction, but he who receives correction is prudent" (Prov. 15:5).

Not only must a prudent man know himself and discipline himself, he must understand the evil that is in the world, and keep himself from it (Prov. 22:3). "A prudent man foreseeth evil and hideth himself; but the simple pass on and are punished" (Prov. 27:12 KJV).

Conclusion

The prudent man not only is wise and knows how to live rightly, he is also able to discipline himself according to what he knows, and directs his life according to the principles he has learned.

ENDNOTES

6. *Webster's New Collegiate Dictionary*, (1976), s. v. "prudence."

7. *Ibid.*, s. v. "prude."

8. *Oxford English Dictionary*, Second Edition (1989), s. v. "prudence."

Proverbs

CHAPTER 14
The Fear of the Lord Leads to Right-Living

Lord, I know wise women strengthen their family,
But foolish women tear it down with foolish actions.

Lord, I will live rightly because I fear You,
But those who live perversely despise You.

Lord, the words I speak will keep me out of trouble,
But the words of a fool become his punishment.

Lord, I'll keep out of trouble if I don't do anything,
But I'll never accomplish anything in life.

Lord, I will not lie,
But a liar will lie with every breath he takes.

Lord, it's easy to find Your wisdom when I search for it,
But scoffers who don't want it can't find it.

Lord, I'll stay away from fools and their influence,
Because I won't hear Your wisdom from them.

Lord, I'll look ahead to see where I'm going,
But the fool deceives himself about right paths.

Lord, I'll come to You to acknowledge my guilt,
But fools make fun of their sin.

Lord, only I know the loneliness of my heart,
And no one else can enter into my feelings.

Lord, You will establish the house of the righteous,
But the home of the wicked will perish.

Lord, each person thinks they choose the right path,
But without You the path leads to death.
People laugh to hide their heavy heart,
But their grief remains when the laughter's over.

Lord, I know You'll reward right living,
But backsliders get what they deserve.

Lord, I will be cautious about every step in life,
But the simple believes everything he hears.

Lord, I will be wise by avoiding danger;
The fool recklessly walks too close to the edge.
He is quick-tempered and makes bad decisions;
He is hated for his sin and stupidity.

Lord, You reward cautious people with good thinking,
But the simpleton gets grief and failure.

Lord, eventually the evil person will recognize my good thinking,
But I'll be within the gates of Heaven
And they'll be in Hell.

Lord, the rich have many outward friends,
While the poor are hated by their neighbors.
Those who despise others, sin against You;
But You bless those who show compassion.

84

Lord, You give me grace when I plan to do good,
But those who plot evil will go astray.
Those who work hard get ahead,
While those who only talk get nothing.
I will be rewarded for my hard work,
But fools are rewarded with foolishness.

Lord, I will help others by telling the truth,
But a liar is a traitor to everyone he speaks to.

Lord, I am secure because I fear You,
And my children also enjoy Your refuge.
I drink the goodness of life from Your fountain,
And escape the temptations that lead to death.

Lord, a wise leader attracts many followers,
But a lesser following shows his influence is declining.

Lord, I am very wise when I control my anger;
Those with quick tempers make foolish mistakes.
Because I keep a tranquil spirit, I'll be healthy,
But those with envy and hate will rot away.

Lord, I will honor You by having mercy on the needy,
But You are insulted by those who oppress the poor.
I will be confident when I face my death,
But the wicked will be judged by their wrong doings.

Lord, I will think right to guarantee my success,
But the fool will fail because he will not think right.
Righteousness makes a nation great,
But sin will always be a snare to any people.
The leader likes those who think right and act right,
But is irritated with those who make bad decisions.
Amen

Proverbs

CHAPTER 15
A Cheerful Heart Leads to Right-Believing

Lord, help me remember that a soft answer turns away anger,
But angry words stir up anger.
Help me wisely use all I've learned
And not be like the fool who spouts foolishness.

Lord, I know Your eyes are everywhere,
Seeing both evil and good actions.
Help my words give life and health to others,
And may they not deceitfully crush the spirit of people.
Help me learn wisdom when I am corrected
And not be like the fool who despises his parents' discipline.
May my house be filled with the treasures of wisdom,
And not like the rebels who get trouble from their money.

Lord, help me give good advice to others,
Because fools do not have wisdom to share with friends.
I know You delight in the prayers of righteous people,
But reject good works by wicked people.
I know You love those who pursue right-living
And despise the wickedness of the wicked.

Lord, You discipline those who forsake Your straight path,
And they will die by refusing Your correction.
Because You know what's in death and Hell,
How much more You know what's in the human heart.

Lord, because a scorner won't listen to corrections
He won't go to the wise for advice.

Lord, I have a happy face because my heart rejoices,
But a scorner breaks the human spirit.
Give me an inquiring mind so I can become wise;
I don't want to be like a fool who feeds on foolishness.

Lord, every day You set a new table before me,
But the scorner is daily stressed with affliction.
I would rather have little food and fear You
Than have plenty to eat and a life of trouble.
Better a bowl of vegetable soup with someone you love
Than a sirloin steak with someone you hate.

Lord, I will be a peace-maker,
Because quick-tempered people disrupt things.
I will be diligent so my path will be easy,
Because the slothful allows thorns to grow over everything.

Lord, I will make my parents proud of me,
Because the rebellious son shows he hates his parents.
I will live sensibly and stay on the right track,
Even when fools find happiness in being foolish.
I will need the help of good counselors to make good plans,
Because plans go astray without wise advice.

Lord, help me always say the right thing at the right time,
Because people listen to a fitting reply.
I will follow the path that leads to life above,
And avoid the rebellious ways that lead to Hell.

Lord, You destroy the things of arrogant people
Who think they've made it by themselves;
And You protect the property of widows.

I hate the thought of taking or giving bribes,
Because wicked money earned by wicked acts troubles the family.

Lord, You delight when I speak right words the right way,
But You despise the wicked thoughts of the wicked.
I will think about my answers before speaking,
Because evil people only spew out evil words.

Lord, You hear the prayers of right-acting people,
But You shut up Your ears to the wicked.
I'm happy when I see an optimistic glance in the eyes of another,
Because good news lifts my spirit.

I will be comfortable around wise people,
Because I want to learn from their counsel.
I will grow in understanding when I listen to the wise,
But a man hurts himself when he doesn't listen to others.

Lord, reverencing You is the first step to successful believing
And I must be humble before I receive honor.
Amen

CHAPTER 16
The Lord's Providential Care

Lord, I will carefully discipline my speech,
So I trust You to help me give the right answers.
Every man justifies his actions in his mind,
But You, Lord, know the real motives of my heart.

Lord, when I will commit myself to think right,
My actions will be successful.
You have a purpose for me in all You create and do,
You even punish the wicked for a purpose.
If I think I am better than You, that is an abomination;
That attitude will not escape punishment
Even if rebels bands with others who hate You.
You punish by the standards of truth and consistency;
I will reverence You to escape punishment.

Lord, when my actions please You
My enemies cannot accuse me of anything.
I would rather live right and have little gain
Than draw a huge salary from sinful acts.

Lord, I make plans in the integrity of my heart,
But You direct each step I take.
You direct my life through government authorities;
It's very difficult to go against their decisions.
You want me to be honest in everything I count,
Because You know the correct measure of all things.

Lord, it is an abomination when government authorities do wrong,
Because You established their authority so people can live by laws.
Government officials expect everyone to keep the peace
And their job is easier when everyone lives by the law.
But government officials punish when they are mad,
So I will not anger them.
I'm fortunate when governmental officials smile at me,
Because they can be as beneficial as an autumn rain.

Lord, I would rather have a good mind than great riches
And I would rather think successfully than get wealth.
I will walk the right way and turn my back on evil
To preserve my soul.

Lord, pride will trip me up in many ways
And a rebellious spirit will destroy me.
I would rather spend my life with humble people
Than get rich with a lot of haughty rebellious people.

Lord, I want the good results that come
from handling problems wisely,
Because I will be happy doing things Your way.
I want to be wise with a reputation for self-discipline,
And I want my optimism to motivate others to learn.
I want to think right so I can live successfully,
But to fools thinking right is foolishness.

Lord, to think right begins with a choice to be wise
And it will show when I speak.
Good words are the source of a happy life
And they give life to the whole body.

Lord, each person thinks they choose the right path,
But without You the path leads to death.

Lord, I work because it reflects who I am;
But it's also a means to provide my livelihood.

Lord, sinners are always thirsting for more sin;
But their lips are burned when they drink it.
A deceitful person makes everyone mad
And a gossip drives a wedge between friends.
A violent man will challenge his friends to a fight
And make them do things they don't want to do.
He shuts his eyes to the truth, and criticizes everything
Using his lips to get his evil way.

Lord, I want to glorify You in my old age;
Because I've always thought right to live successfully.
When I keep my temper and not blow my stack,
I will be mightier than the mighty.
When I conquer my inner spirit,
I will be like those who conquer a city.

Lord, life is like the rolling of the dice,
But You determine what will happen to all.
Amen

CHARACTER SKETCH:

The Scoffer

"A proud [and] haughty [man] – "Scoffer" [is] his name; He acts with arrogant pride" (Prov. 21:24). "The devising of fool-ishness [is] sin, and the scoffer [is] an abomination to men" (Prov. 24:9). "A scoffer seeks wisdom and does not [find it,]" (Prov. 14:6). "A scoffer does not love one who corrects him, nor will he go to the wise" (Prov. 15:12). "Strike a scoffer, and the simple will become wary; rebuke one who has understand-ing, [and] he will discern knowledge;" "Judgments are pre-pared for scoffers, and beatings for the backs of fools" (Prov. 19:25,29). "When the scoffer is punished, the simple is made wise" (Prov. 21:11). "Scoffers set a city aflame, but wise [men] turn away wrath" (Prov. 29:8).

The scoffer actually falls under the category of a fool, but he expresses his arrogance in criticism, negative responses, mockery, or showing contempt for others. The scoffer is proud, and thinks that he is always right. *Webster* defines a scoffer as, "to treat or address with derision."9

The scoffer's problem is pride, arrogance, and self-centeredness. According to the Proverbs, "A proud [and] haughty [man] – "Scoffer" [is] his name; he acts with arrogant pride" (Prov. 21:24). He is called proud, a haughty person. "Only by pride cometh contention: but with the well advised [is] wisdom" (Prov. 13:10 KJV).

The scoffer criticizes others because he thinks his actions or decisions are better than anyone else's. He is negative because he thinks he is right and everyone else is wrong. The scoffer's problem is not seeing the contribution of others. It's his perfectionist nature; the scoffer criticizes because he is blinded by his pride, and feels he is better than anyone else.

A scoffer has difficulty learning anything. Because he is a grouch and critic, he can't look on the good side of anything, nor can he learn right principles to guide his life. He will not listen to others, nor is he tolerant of their point of view. "A scoffer does not love one who corrects him, nor will he go to the wise" (Prov. 15:12).

Even when a scoffer says he wants to learn something, it's difficult for him to apply it to his life because he feels his way of doing things is best. "A scoffer seeks wisdom and does not [find it,]" (Prov. 14:6).

A scoffer thinks he is wise. Because of his wrong impression of his own abilities, the scoffer cannot learn. "Do you see a man wise in his own eyes? [There is] more hope for a fool than for him" (Prov. 26:12). If a conceited man thinks he knows everything, who can teach him anything?

The scoffer creates trouble for himself. Because the scoffer thinks he is always right, he can't see right principles nor live by them. He constantly tears down anything that disagrees with his orientation to life; he is not a builder of things. He doesn't build up himself, he doesn't build up his family, nor does he build up his friends. The scoffer who thinks he knows it all actually can't listen to those who want to help him, nor will he listen to Christian leaders who try to correct him or give him God's principles by which he should live. "Scornful men bring a city into a snare: but wise [men] turn away wrath" (Prov. 29:8 KJV).

Don't let a scorner ruin your life. Don't allow scorners to have any place in your life, "Cast out the scorner, and contention shall go out; yea, strife and reproach shall cease" (Prov. 22:10 KJV).

How can a scorner become wise? He must quit complaining and griping. Notice what the wise people do, "but wise [men] turn away wrath" (Prov. 29:8). This means those who live by right principles will be peacemakers. So when a scorner begins practicing the role of peacemaker, they begin taking steps to become wise.

The scoffer is headed toward punishment or destruction. "Pride [goeth] before destruction, and an haughty spirit before a fall" (Prov. 16:18 KJV). One of the problems with pride is that it creates a false security in the scoffer; when in fact, they suffer the consequences from their own ignorance. And who is the rebel? One who has more confidence in his ability to run his life than he has in someone else, or in God's ability to guide him by right principles. Self-will and rebellion go hand in hand, "An high look, and a proud heart, [and] the plowing of the wicked, [is] sin" (Prov. 21:4).

Conclusion

The scoffer has a negative attitude toward everyone and everything in life—except himself. His problem is his inability to see truth and apply it to his life. Because the scoffer will not embrace wisdom (right-believing), he does not have the ability to believe himself to success.

ENDNOTE

9. *Merriam Webster Online Dictionary,* http://www.m-w.com/cgi-bin/dictionary?book=Dictionary&va=scoffer, <accessed 16 February 2005>.

CHAPTER 17
A Fool Doesn't Believe Right

Lord, I'd rather eat a simple sandwich in peace
Than have the best banquet where hate is prevalent.
A wise employee who controls a rebellious son
Will be rewarded with those who are faithful.
We have standards to test the purity of gold and silver,
But only You honestly test the hearts of people.
Rebels are influenced by wicked conversation;
Liars pay attention to gross exaggerations.

Lord, those mocking the poor make fun of You who made all people;
Those who rejoice at the accident of others will suffer accidents.

Lord, grandchildren are our prize for getting older,
And the pride of children is their parents and grandparents.
Fools do not speak properly
And lying leaders are even more foolish.

Lord, I will get good will when I give a gift
If I give the gift in good faith.
My love to another is strengthened when I overlook his faults;
Pointing out his problems separates the best of friends.
I will learn even from rebels because I want to succeed,
But a fool won't listen if you tell him 100 times.
Those who break rules are rebellious in their heart;
They will only learn from the cruel consequences of their mistakes.
It's safer to meet a bear robbed of its cubs

Than deal with a fool in his foolishness.
Lord, those who give evil to people who do them good
Will have more evil than they can bear;
They will never get rid of evil.
Those who start a fight are like those who open the flood gates;
It's hard to stop a flood once it gets going
And it's hard to stop quarreling once it gets started.
Those who excuse the rebel and condemn the righteous
Are both an abomination to You.
A fool won't pay tuition for a college education,
Because he doesn't want to learn anything.

Lord, I will have my friends at all times;
That is one of my purposes in life.

Lord, if I guarantee a loan for someone
I am responsible for his debts.
Those who enjoy arguing, also enjoy sinning;
And those who brag about their strengths invite attacks.
Those with twisted ideas do not try to live right,
And those with twisted tongues end up in trouble.
It is painful to a parent to let their children become fools,
And a parent is not proved
When their child won't think right.

Lord, my rejoicing heart is good medicine,
But a broken heart makes me feel bad all over.
The rebel will accept illegal bribes
To cover a lie or pervert justice.

Lord, help me think right so I can live successfully;
I don't want to be distracted by worldly traps.
A foolish child who won't listen to right-thinking
Angers a good father,
And embitters his mother who gave him birth;

But to punish the innocent is wrong,
Likewise to punish leaders who do right.

Lord, help me to use my knowledge to discipline my speech;
Because wise people control their temper
And a fool is thought wise if he doesn't speak;
So others who keep their mouths shut
Will appear to be wise to everyone.
Amen

Proverbs

CHAPTER 18
A Contrast Between Perils and Blessings

Lord, I don't want to be a recluse or hermit;
They selfishly think only of themselves
And deny every principle of getting along with people.
A fool never tries to learn from others,
They only want to arrogantly express their advice.
A wicked person brings rebellion into the room,
Then provocation and arguments follow.

Lord, I want my words to give the water of life,
Flowing out to refresh everyone I encounter.

Lord, it is wrong to reward the wicked
And condemn those who do the right things.
A fool gets into fights because of what he says,
But it's his evil heart that gets him beat up.
The mouth of a fool keeps him in constant trouble;
He can't do right because his words continually trip him up.
Gossip is slippery sweet like honey,
It'll slip into the belly and make you sick.

Lord, a lazy man who never accomplishes anything
Is as bad as one who destroys what others accomplish.

Lord, wealthy people believe their riches are their defense;
They believe money is their fortification.

But Your name is a strong tower;
I will run to You for safety.

Lord, I know proud people will eventually be destroyed,
So, make me humble so I can be successful.
Help me listen carefully to matters before I answer,
Because it's foolish to give the wrong answers.

Lord, I can make it through sickness when I think right;
But I give up when my spirit is deflated.
I will be wise because I want to learn
And I will learn because I've purposed to think right.
Giving to people is a way to influence them
And brings me before influential people.
The first thing I hear usually seems to be right
Until someone straightens the record with the truth.
Drawing straws can settle arguments
Because neither person has to give in;
Yet, one person is the winner.
It's harder to win back the friendship of an offended brother
Than to win a big physical fight,
Because the offense is taken to heart.
Good food in the mouth satisfies the belly
Just like good words make the spirit happy.

Lord, teach me to discipline my speech
Because the tongue can kill or nourish life.

Lord, the man who finds a good wife
Discovers the greatest treasure to possess;
And he gets Your blessing in life.
The poor always beg and need some help,
But the rich seem to speak straightforwardly.
A man must be friendly to have friends,
And You are the friend that is closer than a brother.
Amen

CHARACTER SKETCH:
The Righteous

"The righteousness of the upright will deliver them" (Prov. 11:6). "And the desire of the righteous will be granted" (Prov. 10:24). "The labor of the righteous [leads] to life" (Prov. 10:16). "Righteousness [leads] to life" (Prov. 11:19).

One of the most common descriptions of people in Proverbs is those who live for God. Proverbs calls them, *the righteous.* In the New Testament, the righteous are those who have been declared righteous through their faith in Jesus Christ (Rom. 3:24,25). But in Proverbs the righteous are those who live by the right principles. Proverbs doesn't point out right principles by quoting other books of the Bible. The *right principles* of the righteous are those that have been learned by observation of life, i.e., common sense.

The Book of Proverbs describes the righteous prospering, but the wicked eventually end up destroying themselves. However, there is no automatic guarantee that every person who lives by right principles can manipulate his circumstances to achieve the wealth or get what they desire. Some people who live by right principles are not financially successful, and they never seem to enjoy material benefits in life. Look at Job: he was righteous, yet he suffered many afflictions.

The Book of Proverbs contains observations that most wicked people suffer the consequences of their rebellion. But, some wicked people seem to live on "easy street." They never seem to have any apparent reverses. However, Proverbs adds a time element and eventually the wickedness of the wicked catches up, and the right-living of the right-eous will lead them to prosperity.

But even though some righteous may suffer and some wicked may prosper, as a general rule, those who live by the right principles are more successful, more happy, and have better lives than those who rebel against their parents and eventually rebel against God. Why? Because those who rebel against any laws will eventually rebel against all laws. They will rebel against government rules, against the principles of common sense concerning finances, health and family relationships. As a result, the rebels usually fail in their endeavor; they never achieve their goals, and they are more miserable with their circumstances than the righteous.

The righteous person has more confidence and security. "He who walks with integrity walks securely" (Prov. 10:9). Therefore, those who follow right principles are not plagued by fear, nor are they "dogged" by self doubt. The righteous enjoy their integrity, "The integrity of the upright will guide them" (Prov. 11:3). That means they do not have to deal with guilt, nor do they have to worry about what people think about them.

Living by right principles leads to success and advancement. "The righteousness of the upright will deliver them" (Prov. 11:6). That means the principles they follow will lead them to success.

Those who live by right principles please God. "[The] blameless in their ways [are] His delight" (Prov. 11:20). While doing the right thing is the focus of Proverbs, in the New Testament it is your absolute trust or faith that pleases God. "But without faith [it is] impossible to please [Him,] for he who comes to God must believe that He is, and [that] He is a rewarder of those who diligently seek Him" (Heb. 11:6).

Those who live by right principles usually accomplish the desires of their heart, "And the desire of the righteous will be granted" (Prov. 10:24). This doesn't mean that Christians can get everything that they want; no, look at the process by which we desire things. Those who do right will probably desire what is right in God's sight. They will not be doing selfish things or sinful things; therefore, because they want what God desires for them, and they live according to God's principles, they accomplish their desires in life. This is another way of saying, "Delight thyself also in the Lord; and he shall give thee the desires of thine heart" (Ps. 37:4 KJV).

Those who live by right principles enjoy the fullness of life. When the righteous work by right principles, "The labor of the righteous [leads] to life" (Prov. 10:16). Beyond their work, just living by right principles gives them a full life, "Righteousness [leads] to life" (Prov. 11:19), and they enjoy the promise, "No grave trouble will overtake the righteous" (Prov. 12:21) because their conscience is clear. Because they're doing what they desire, they find much to sing about and praise God. A man was constantly asked, "How are you today?" He always answered, "Rejoicing!"

In spite of reversals and problems those who live by right principles will eventually get up and overcome their problems. Proverbs teaches, "For a righteous [man] may fall seven times and rise again" (Prov. 24:16). He has the eternal stamina to keep on going because he knows his case is just. He has the ability to overcome obstacles because he is living and working by right principles. Because his principles will eventually prevail, the righteous man keeps doing the right thing.

Conclusion

The book of Proverbs wants every person to be wise. That means they believe right, live by right principles, and do the right thing. Those who fall short of living by right principles are called simpletons, fools, sluggards, etc. Those who live by the current principles taught in Proverbs save themselves a lot of grief and have productive, happy lives.

Proverbs

Chapter 19

Build Character by Wise-Believing

Lord, I'd rather be poor and live morally upright
Than be a fool and morally dishonest.
It's not wise to act impulsively without knowing what I'm doing;
I'd rush ahead without knowing where I'm going.
A fool is ruined by his own foolishness,
Then angrily blames God for his failure.
Wealthy people appear to have many "friends,"
While the poor have only a few.
Lies will always add grief to the liar;
He will not escape his punishment.
Many people want something from their leaders;
They are his friend to get something.
The relatives of a poor man despise him,
And his friends ignore him.
When the poor man needs them and calls to them
They don't respond to his requests.

Lord, I have enough self-respect to get wisdom
And I will prosper because of right-believing.
Those who put up a false front will be embarrassed,
And those who tell lies will be punished.

Lord, it's wrong for a fool to live in the lap of luxury,
And for jail inmates to tell presidents what to do.

Lord, I'll discipline my anger because I want to be wise,
And I'll overlook the mistakes of others.
The king's wrath terrifies like the roar of a lion,
But his favor is like dew on the grass.
A foolish son will disillusion his father,
And a nagging wife irritates her husband
Like a faucet that keeps dripping.

Lord, a house and wealth are inherited from Your family,
But You give a wife who thinks sensibly.
A lazy person sleeps instead of working,
And as a result, goes hungry.

Lord, I live correctly when I obey your commandments;
Those who despise Your way of life will die.

Lord, I'm lending to You when I help the poor;
I know You will repay in many ways.
I will discipline my children while they can learn
So their life won't be ruined.
A violent-tempered person will pay for his anger;
You can try to stop him from getting mad
But You'll have to do it again.

Lord, I will obey good advice and learn from discipline
So I'll have a good life, for the rest of my life.

Lord, I can make any plans in my heart,
But Your purpose in life will prevail.

Lord, I will be loyal so I can influence people,
And I'd rather be poor than get money by lying.

Lord, I will reverently trust You for eternal life,
And evil will not be able to touch me.
Some lazy people are so lazy

That they will not lift a hand to feed themselves.
When the rebellious person is punished,
The simpleton can learn from that example.
When the wise are corrected, they learn valuable lessons.
The children who mistreat their father or reject their mother
Are a disgrace and embarrassment to them.

Lord, when I stop listening to correction,
I have turned my back on common sense.
A lying witness makes a mockery of justice,
And wicked people drink in evil.
The scorner will be judged for his scorn,
Just as surely as fools will be judged.
Amen

Proverbs

CHAPTER 20
Build a Life of Integrity

Lord, wine makes a mockery of wise people,
and liquor leads to fights;
I will not be led astray by using it.

Lord, the leader's anger is like a lion's roar;
Those who make him mad risk their lives.

Lord, I will become wise by avoiding quarrels,
Any fool can fly off the handle in rage.

Lord, those who are too lazy to plow in the spring
Won't have any food in the harvest.

Lord, my intentions lie deep within my heart;
But a wise person can know what I'm thinking.

Lord, many people announce they are my good friends;
But only the faithful ones stick with me.

Lord, I want to think right and walk in integrity
So my children may happily follow my example.

Lord, I want to look at all the evidence
Before I decide if something is good or bad.

Lord, I cannot say I am pure from all sin;
No one can cleanse themselves from iniquity.

Lord, I know You hate double standards and price fixing,
So padding an expense account and lying about taxes is wrong.

Lord, I want to be innocent and transparent like a child,
So everyone will know the purity of my heart.

Lord, I want to hear what You made the ears to hear
And see what You made the eyes to see.

Lord, I will not spend my days sleeping;
But will open my eyes to the tasks before me,
So my needs will be supplied.

Lord, I will not bad-mouth a product to get a better price,
Then go off and brag that I got a bargain.

Lord, I don't want just gold and jewels,
I want to be wise in discernment and decision-making.

Lord, I will get collateral before making a loan;
I will need security when making a loan to a stranger.

Lord, when I steal or lie to get something illegally,
It will turn sour in my stomach.

Lord, I will make good plans to have success in life;
And I'll seek advice when attempting something big.

Lord, I know a gossiper goes around telling secrets,
So she can't tell anything I don't tell her.

Lord, those who curse their father and mother,
Their lamp will be put out and they'll be in darkness.

Lord, when I get a possession too soon, and too easily
I usually don't appreciate it in the long run.

Lord, I won't give a bad deed in return for evil;
Rather, I'll wait for You to punish the evil doer.

Lord, You hate a double standard that gives some an advantage,
And You despise double entry bookkeeping.

Lord, You order the steps of a good man;
So, help me know how to walk properly.

Lord, it is a sin to pledge money to You
Then change the mind and not give it.

Lord, help me be a wise leader
to determine who is violating the rules,
Then fire them before they do more damage.

Lord, Your searchlight penetrates my human heart
To expose all the reasons for my actions.

Lord, Your grace and truth put the king on the throne;
Your mercy keeps him there.

Lord, the glory of a youth is his strength;
The splendor of the elderly is their experience and wisdom.

Lord, I know physical punishment will deal with disobedience
If it deals with the heart, not just the body.
Amen

The Shrew

(The Scolding Wife)

"It is better to dwell in a corner of the housetop, than with a brawling woman in a wide house" (Prov. 21:9 KJV). "A continual dripping on a very rainy day and a contentious woman are alike" (Prov. 27:15).

A shrew is the traditional word to describe a scolding, fussing, bitter, complaining wife. It's an Old English word that meant a woman who was ill-tempered and mean. If her husband was hen-pecked, she does the pecking. Another old term was vixen, but the worst thing about a shrew is that the word comes from *shrewe* which means evil or cursed. A man with an ill-tempered wife is cursed to a life of misery. Solomon, who married many women, probably had a few wives he would describe as shrews. He described a good-looking woman without discretion as a golden jewel in a pig's snout (Prov. 11:22). That's like saying a beautiful woman with an evil disposition is as out of place as a diamond earring on a pig.

Also, Solomon was probably speaking from experience when he said, "It is better to dwell in a corner of the housetop, than with a brawling woman in a wide house" (Prov. 21:9 KJV). We can imagine Solomon's palace was big or "a wide house." He was willing to give up his palace, "It is better to dwell in the wilderness, than with a contentious and an angry woman" (Prov. 21:19 KJV). He must have had some wives who were ill-tempered, sarcastic and perhaps vitriolic and even blasphemous.

The problem with the contentious woman was not her rash anger, or an occasional emotional blowout; a contentious woman uses every opportunity to criticize, to blame, and tear down her husband. She is outwardly angry because she is inwardly bitter and revengeful. "A continual dripping on a very rainy day and a contentious woman are alike" (Prov. 27:15).

Solomon noted, "For three [things] the earth is perturbed, yes, for four it cannot bear up" (Prov. 30:21). The third thing on his list to avoid was an "odious woman" (Prov. 30:23 KJV), which the *New Living Translation* translates "a bitter woman." Solomon seems to be saying, don't marry a bitter, complaining woman, because love won't make any difference in the relationship. Since the mouth always speaks from the heart, she will continually nag her husband if her heart is angry.

Conclusion

The contentious shrew is not the evil, whorish woman who is called a trollop. No, the trollop has beautiful speech and sets an alluring atmosphere to trap a man and tempt him to have sex with her. The shrew has an opposite approach. She constantly fusses at her husband if he looks at another woman, or even speaks to another woman. The shrew is suspicious that her husband has been unfaithful to her, and criticizes him to family and friends. The shrew makes life miserable for anyone with whom she comes in contact.

CHAPTER 21
Build a Life-Plan

Lord, the king's heart is in Your hand like a river,
You turn it wherever You please.

Lord, many think they are doing the right thing,
But You know the truth found in each heart.

Lord, You are more pleased when I do the right things,
Than when I give You a gift of sacrifice.

Lord, haughty eyes and an arrogant attitude is just as much sin
As all the actions that break Your law.

Lord, I will succeed with good planning and hard work,
But, will fail when I goof off and give it my second best.
And wealth gotten by lying will vanish like the early fog;
It is a sedative trap that leads to death.
Also, the violence of the wicked will destroy them
Because they refuse to do the right thing.

Lord, I know the rebel walks a rebellious path;
But those who believe right will walk right.

Lord, I'd rather live on a small corner of a roof
Than share a large house with a nagging wife.

Lord, evil people love to do evil things;
They have no consideration for their neighbors.

Lord, when a scorner is punished, the simpleton learns to think right;
When the wise is instructed, he learns to live right.

Lord, You know what happens in the home of the wicked,
And eventually You will judge their wickedness
Those who shut their ears to the requests of the poor
Will be ignored when their time of need comes.
A personal gift gets favor to the giver,
But a bribe under the table will be punished.

Lord, I enjoy right-living because I practice right-thinking;
And this righteousness terrifies the evil doers.

Lord, the one who strays from the path of common sense
Will end up dead like others who violated Your law.
The ones given to pleasure shall end up poor,
And the ones given to wine will never succeed.

Lord, sometimes You punish the wicked to save the upright,
And You judge the treacherous to pressure the godly.
It is better to live alone in the desert
Than to live with a complaining, negative wife.

Lord, the wise have a nice home and furnishings,
But a fool spends his money as soon as he gets it.

Lord, when I seek to believe right and live right
You've promised me life, wisdom and honor.
The wise can conquer strong warriors,
Because he uses wisdom to undermine their fortifications.

116

Lord, when I discipline my thinking and words
I will stay out of trouble.
Those who are guided by overwhelming conceit
Are arrogant rebels of Your expectations.
The craving of a lazy man will eat him up,
Because he is too lazy to work for the things he wants.
He is greedy but will not pay the price,
But the righteous have something to give.

Lord, You hate the good works of rebellious people;
Especially when they do them with ulterior motives.
A lying witness will eventually be punished,
But those who know the truth will be allowed to speak.
A wicked man covers up his real feelings,
But the upright plans to live right.

Lord, no human plans that are made against You
Will succeed in the long run.
The battle armaments are prepared for war,
But You are the One who gives victory.
Amen

Proverbs

CHAPTER 22
What to Avoid in Life

Lord, I would rather have a good reputation than lots of money;
I want respect more than silver or gold.
The rich and the poor have one thing in common,
You made them both.

Lord, a wise man sees problems coming and gets out of the way,
But problems run over the naïve, then he suffers the consequences.

Lord, when I fear You, I have a proper view of myself
And I will be properly equipped to make money.

Lord, stubborn people will run into a lot of difficulties,
But those who believe-right will be able to avoid them.

Lord, if I properly train a child to believe and act right,
He will live-right when he grows up.

Lord, those who break the law end up in trouble,
And it will do them no good to get angry.

Lord, those who have a generous spirit add value to their life
Because they share with the needy.

Lord, kick the sarcastic person out and people will stop fussing;
Also, they will stop giving one another insults.

Lord, those who are conscientious and give compliments
Will get the attention of the boss.

Lord, You protect the wise right-believing person,
And You upset the schemes of schemers.

Lord, the lazy man makes up hypothetical problems,
Complaining there's a lion in the street;
All because he's too lazy to do anything.

Lord, the mouth of the adulteress is a deep hole;
Those who are angry with the Lord fall into it.

Lord, it's natural for a foolish child to do stupid things;
He needs to be corrected to live a wise life.
It's not smart to make money off the poor,
And you'll lose the money you give to the rich.

Lord, I will pay attention when the wise instruct me
So I can gain knowledge and wisdom.
Because when I have the principles of wise people in my heart,
I can explain why I live by God's rules.
I will put my trust in the Lord alone,
And I then can tell others how to live for You.

Lord, Solomon has given us these worthwhile principles
To instruct us how to live and to keep us out of trouble,
So I can live with Your assurance,
And tell others how You expect them to live.

Lord, I will not take advantage of the helpless
who cannot help themselves,
And I won't sue the poor to get my money
Because You watch out for the poor,
And withhold blessings from those who oppress them.

Lord, I will not hang out with angry people
Nor become close friends with hot-heads
Because being around them will make me become like them,
And I'll suffer the consequences of their mean-spiritedness.

Lord, I won't sign loan papers for those who ask me
To guarantee a loan for them
Because I'll eventually have to pay for them;
And if I don't have the money to pay their loan,
My house and furniture will be repossessed.

Lord, I won't move the ancient boundary markers
That were set up by the ancestors;
Because the stability of the past guarantees my future.

Lord, I want to be the most skilled at what I do
So I will be recognized and promoted.
Amen

CHARACTER SKETCH:

The Drunkard

"Do not mix with winebibbers" (Prov. 23:20). "Do not look on the wine when it is red, when it sparkles in the cup, [when] it swirls around smoothly" (Prov. 23:31).

What does the Book of Proverbs mean when it describes the drunk? Is this someone who takes a social drink, or is it someone who gets dead drunk, or is it an alcoholic, i.e., someone addicted to alcohol?

Webster defines these three positions of drunk: First, "Having the facilities impaired by alcohol."[10] The second, "One given over to habitual excessive use of alcohol."[11] And third, "The drunk is the one suffering from or subject to acute or chronic drunkenness," [12] i.e., he is addicted.

The Book of Proverbs gives a clear command to stay away from drunkenness by staying away from those who drink, "Do not mix with winebibbers" (Prov. 23:20). This means don't hang around people drinking alcohol, i.e., social drinkers.

Notice the long explanation of the drunk in Proverbs:

"Who has anguish? Who has sorrow? Who is always fighting? Who is always complaining? Who has unnecessary bruises? Who has bloodshot eyes? It is the one who spends long hours in the taverns, trying out new drinks. Don't let the sparkle and smooth taste of wine deceive you. For in the end it bites like a poisonous serpent; it stings like a viper. You will see hallucinations, and you will say crazy things. You will stagger like a sailor tossed at sea, clinging to a swaying mast. And you will say, 'They hit me, but I didn't feel it. I didn't even know it when they beat me up. When will I wake up so I can have another drink?'" (Prov. 23:29-35 NLT).

Since the diligent person has self-discipline, the drunk is never described as a diligent person—the drunk is controlled by the spirit of the bottle. Also, the drunk is not a wise person, for the wise person thinks rightly, and the drunk does not think rightly. Finally, the drunk cannot be righteous, because the righteous person lives by principles, and the drunk does not. Rather, the drunk lives to please the flesh as does the fool. The drunk lives for self-satisfaction as does the sluggard. There is nothing about the drunk that is desirable.

When Proverbs asks the question, "Who has unnecessary bruises?" (Prov. 23:29 NLT), it suggests that the drunkard might have avoided his wounds. Specifically, his wounds are self-inflicted. Those who give themselves over to wine take to themselves poison, such as being bitten by a snake that will lead to death. Alcohol is described here as poison.

The drunk may lose control of his consciousness; but more importantly, he loses control of his morals. His speech is confused and he staggers when he walks. Proverbs says the walk of the drunk is like walking on a ship in the midst of a raging storm (Prov. 23:34). The drunken person's senses are so blunted that he could be beaten and not remember the pain. "They have struck me, [but] I was not hurt; they have beaten me, but I did not feel [it]" (Prov. 23:35). And what is the future of the drunk? He lives for the bottle and the momentary pleasure it gives. Or he lives for the escapism from life's problems. "When shall I awake, that I may seek another [drink]?" (Prov. 23:35) The drunk is addicted to the wine, and its destructive addiction will eventually destroy his life.

Conclusion

The Book of Proverbs does not allow for social drinking or drinking alcohol in any form. Those who are foolish deserve all subsequent consequences of choosing drunkenness. When Proverbs describes alcohol as the poison of a serpent or adder, it is saying one drop of poison will kill, so stay completely away.

ENDNOTES

10. *Webster's New Collegiate Dictionary* (1976), s. v. "drunk."
11. *Webster's Third International Dictionary,* unabridged (1993), s. v. "drunken."
12. *Ibid.*, s. v. "drunkard."

Proverbs

CHAPTER 23

Don't Lust for the Things That Evil People Get by Doing Evil

Lord, help me when I sit to eat with leaders
To remember who I am with.
Help me not to gorge my stomach with food
So that I don't embarrass myself.
Help me not to lust after delicacies;
Because being greedy reveals my lack of character
And is not healthy and nourishing.

Lord, help me not to exhaust my strength pursuing money,
But be smart enough to control myself.
Help me not set my eyes on riches,
For I'll lose sight of everything else in life.
Wealth is an elusive goal that has the wings of a bird;
Just when you think you have it, off it flies.

Lord, I'll not eat the food of a stingy man,
Nor be greedy for the delicacies of his table;
For he keeps count of all I eat.
He says to me, "Eat and drink," but he doesn't mean it.
For that which I eat, I'll have to repay;
My compliments for his meal will be wasted.

Lord, I'll not quietly correct a fool
For he will despise the common sense I tell him.

Lord, I won't move the ancient boundary stones
To encroach on the property of another;
For You, Lord, are our Redeemer
And You may take up the fight against us.

Lord, I will discipline my mind to learn knowledge
And listen to hear words of wisdom;
I'll not withhold discipline from a child
For if I correct him he will not die;
But with correction he will learn wisdom and live.

Lord, I want my children to learn wisdom
So that I'll be glad when they speak wise words;
My heroes will not be those who despise Your law.

Lord, I'll follow the example of those who follow You;
For a solid future is with those who fear You,
And I'll not be cut down in the prime of life.

Lord, I'll listen to wise men and become wise;
I'll set my mind on the right kind of life.

Lord, I'll not be addicted to guzzling strong drink,
Nor will I eat like a pig;
For both the drunkard and glutton will become poor
And laziness will only buy rags to wear.

Lord, I'll listen to my father who gave me life
And I'll honor my mother all of her life long.

Lord, I'll give my money to get as much truth as possible,
And with it I'll get discipline, understanding, and wisdom.

Lord, the father of a right-living son will rejoice
And a wise son will make him glad.

So I will make my father and mother rejoice;
They will be proud of me as their child.

Lord, I give You my heart to control my life;
Let my eyes see how You want me to live.

Lord, I reject the prostitute who is a deep ditch
And I refuse the trollop who is a narrow well;
They lie in wait to catch straying males,
And like predators, they eat human flesh.

Lord, what idiot has misery? Who has sorrow?
Who gets into quarrels and fights?
Who gets beat up and who has his body bloodied?
Who has bloodshot eyes and a hangover?
Those who can't say "NO!" to liquor or beer,
Those who search for a new mixed drink.

Lord, You tell us to never look with desire into the glass
As it gives off its smell and smooth color.
It may slide smoothly down the throat;
It may seem like a heavenly taste.
But liquor bites like a hidden serpent;
Its sip is the venom of a deadly snake
So I determine never to take my first drink.

Lord, the eyes of a drunken man see peculiar things;
His mind is hopelessly messed up.
He staggers as if he were walking on a rolling ship;
His head heaves as if he's on the top of a mast.
People can beat on him when he's drunk and he'll not feel it;
He'll feel like he's been beaten up after he gets sober.

Lord, the pathetic drunk is addicted because when he gets sober
He asks, "Where can I get another drink?"
Amen

127

Proverbs

CHAPTER **24**
Learn the Right Values in Life

Lord, I won't make evil people my role models,
And I won't hang out with them;
Because they think of ways to break Your law,
And they try to talk others into their transgressions.

Lord, I can build my home on right-living wisdom
And I can make it secure by right-thinking understanding.
I will fill the rooms with knowledge
And furnish it with the best of thoughts.
I want to be wise so I can be strong
So I will increase my strength with knowledge.
For with wise counsel I can conquer my dreams,
And with many wise counselors, I'll achieve my goals.

Lord, wisdom is a wonderful possession, too lofty for a fool.
The wise man doesn't tell people he's wise
But the important people in the city recognize him.

Lord, those who plan to break the law are called schemers;
And people hate the schemers
Because they are fools given over to sin.

Lord, I promise not to faint in the day of conflict;
Give me strength that is strong enough to endure.

Yes, I'll rescue those about to be killed
And I'll save those being dragged off to death.

Lord, some say "We didn't know anything about it!"
Won't You, Who knows the heart, know it?

Lord, You, who expect all to be truthful,
Will repay each one who quits the battle.

Lord, Solomon tells me to eat honey because it is good for me.
The taste of honey is sweet to the tongue.
Therefore, I know that I should get wisdom
because it is good for me;
Its taste is sweet to the desires of the soul;
Wisdom will give me what I hope for.

Lord, You warn the thief not to lurk
near the home of a righteous man,
And never steal his possessions;
Though a righteous man falls seven times,
He will rise up to bring the thief to judgment;
It's the wicked who falls and never gets up.
Lord, I will not rejoice when my enemy falls
And I won't be happy when he has stumbled;
Because my evil rejoicing will displease You,
You might withdraw Your protection from me
And begin protecting my enemy.

Lord, I will not let evil doers upset me,
Nor will I be envious of the actions of the wicked;
For the person who does evil will not enjoy what he does
And his candle will be put out in death.

Lord, I will not get involved with those who fight the government
And I will fear You, Lord, and the rulers.
For judgment will fall quickly on rebels;
No one knows what ruin will ruin their lives.

Lord, I know these are Your principles
That You prepare for the wise;
I will not show partiality to anyone
When I am making decisions or judgments;
I will not tell guilty people, "You're innocent"
Because the public will curse me and nations will hate me.
But when I condemn those who should be condemned,
The reward of doing right will follow;
When I give an honest answer to those who ask,
It's like giving a kiss to those you respect.

Lord, first I'll prepare myself for honest work
And give an honest day's work to my employer;
I'll then build or buy a home.
I'll not be a witness against someone if it's not so;
I would not use my words to deceive listeners;
I'll not say, "I'll do to my neighbor what he does to me,"
Or, "I'll get even when he does me wrong."

Lord, I walked by a field of a lazy man;
It was the garden of a fool.
It was overgrown with vines and briars;
The ground was covered with weeds,
The fence was broken so everyone could wander in or out.
The more I observed the lazy man's field
The deeper became my conviction about hard work;
The lazy enjoys being lazy and resting;
He loves folding his hands and sleeping late;
But poverty follows the lazy man, as sure as night follows day,
And he'll want for food, clothing and shelter
For the rest of his life.
Amen

CHARACTER SKETCH:

The Sluggard

"The lazy man says, 'there is a lion in the way! There is a lion in the streets!' " (Prov. 26:13 NLT). "A lazy [man] buries his hand in the bowl, and will not so much as bring it to his mouth again." (Prov. 19:24). "As vinegar to the teeth, and as smoke to the eyes, so [is] the sluggard to them that send him" (Prov. 10:26 KJV). "The soul of the sluggard desireth, and [hath] nothing" (Prov. 13:4). "The person who labors, labors for himself, for his [hungry] mouth drives him [on.]" (Prov. 16:26). I went by the field of the lazy [man,] And by the vineyard of the man devoid of understanding; and there it was, all overgrown with thorns; its surface was covered with nettles; its stone wall was broken down. When I saw [it,] I considered [it] well; I looked on [it and] received instruction: a little sleep, a little slumber, a little folding of the hands to rest; so shall your poverty come [like] a prowler, and your need like an armed man." (Prov. 24:30-34).

The title sluggard in Proverbs comes from the Hebrew *asel* which means to be slow or sluggish. Many of the modern versions translate this word *lazy*—one who *lacks motivation*. *Webster's* defines lazy as, "not eager or willing to work or exert oneself; indolent; slothful."[13]

Most everyone begins their day by getting out of bed, but not the sluggard. "[As] a door turns on its hinges, So [does] the lazy [man] on his bed" (Prov. 26:14). As a person who is attached to his bed, like a door to its hinge, and as a person continually tosses in his bed, the sluggard never gets up. It's not a case of being tired, or physically unable; the sluggard lacks ambition, has no focus in life, nor does he have the self-discipline necessary to meet the challenges of a new day.

The sluggard says, "[There is] a lion in the road! A fierce lion [is] in the streets!" (Prov 26:13). The writer is poking fun at the sluggard, because he would rather stay inside than go out to meet the day's challenges or do a day's work. So he either imagines or makes up a story that there is grave danger in a lion outside his house. The threat of a lion is a figment of his imagination.

The next picture of the slothful man is that he is too lazy to eat. "The lazy [man] buries his hand in the bowl; it wearies him to bring it back to his mouth" (Prov. 26:15). Again, the Proverbs offer humor, the sluggard may be hungry but is too lazy to take food out of the bowl and place it in his mouth. He cannot achieve what he needs, or what he wants; he's too lazy to do anything.

But the sluggard has more problems than physical inability. He is guilty of arrogance and self-deceit. Proverbs describes him as "The lazy [man is] wiser in his own eyes than seven men who can answer sensibly" (Prov. 26:16). While seven is the number of perfection, in the face of friendly wisdom, the sluggard thinks he is smarter than them all. Again, laziness leads to hunger and depravity (Prov. 19:15).

Throughout Proverbs, the way of the wise is easy because he solves his problems and works to accomplish his goals. However, there are obstacles in the way of the sluggard, "The way of the lazy [man is] like a hedge of thorns, but the way of the upright [is] a highway" (Prov. 15:19).

Why is laziness rejected? It's not just because they live off others, the lazy person harms everyone around him. That's because laziness is one way of refusing to love your neighbor (Matt. 19:19). So, we are to be as kind to others as we are to ourselves. However, the sluggard is not kind to himself or anyone else.

But there is another thing wrong with laziness. God has commanded that all men work, they provide for their family, and they provide for others.

The writer of Proverbs gives an extended description of laziness (Prov. 24:30-32). He describes, "I went by the field of the lazy [man,] and by the vineyard of the man devoid of understanding; and there it was, all overgrown with thorns; its surface was covered with nettles; its stone wall was broken down." Then the writer describes the plight of the sluggard, "A little sleep, a little slumber, a little folding of the hands to rest; so shall your poverty come [like] a prowler, and your need like an armed man" (Prov. 24:33-34).

The writer describes the "field of the slothful" (Prov. 24:30). The word *slothful* in Hebrew means "lacking heart." Therefore, laziness was not a lack of strength or the ability to work, but there was a "lack." Just as a person without a heart is "a low" soul, so the lazy person is empty of character, determination, and vision.

1. Someone has said that the only thing that works in a sluggard is his mind. He constantly thinks of ways to get out of work, rather than constantly looking to do what his mind tells him (Prov. 22:13; 26:13; 28:15; 24:33).

2. The sluggard eventually becomes a fool. Just as the fool is self-deceived and rejects the way of God, so the sluggard continually procrastinates and rationalizes that his way is better than God's way. The diligence of the wise is contrasted with the laziness of the sluggard (Prov. 10:26) and like all other fools, is headed for destruction (Prov. 6:11; 20:34).

The sluggard needs supervision because the sluggard procrastinates and will not carry out his responsibility. Someone must watch over him to make him work. His hunger pangs won't do it, nor will his poverty (Prov. 13:25; 16:26). It will take the whip of the taskmaster (Prov. 12:24). The writer of Proverbs suggests that they should learn from the ant who works diligently without supervision (Prov. 6:6-8).

The sluggard must change his attitude in life, not his job or work habits. The problem with a lazy person is not his work habits or skill, or even his knowledge of what he has to do. The problem with a lazy person is his thinking. The sluggard is self-seeking (Prov. 21:25,26), pleasure-seeking (Prov. 13:4; 21:17) and short-sighted, "He who gathers in summer [is] a wise son; He who sleeps in harvest [is] a son who causes shame" (Prov. 10:5), and lacks self-discipline.

Therefore to change the sluggard, you have to change his way of thinking. The sluggard must say, "I repent of my laziness and I commit myself to working hard." Then the sluggard must go a step further, "I will learn how to work hard; I will learn skills to be protective and I will learn all the knowledge I need to know about my job."

The sluggard does not love or fear God; throughout the book of Proverbs he is contrasted with the righteous (Prov. 15:19; 21:25-26) and he is assumed to be wicked (Prov. 13:25). Those who have no regard for God's will or for their life neither have any regard for their fellow man.

Next, the sluggard must change his entire value system. His previous life's goal was to be happy, now it must change to life by God's principles. Not to be prosperous (Prov. 30:7) but to please God and give according to the principles of God.

Finally, the sluggard must stop running, talking and thinking about work; he must go to work. "He who tills his land will be satisfied with bread, But he who follows frivolity [is] devoid of understanding" (Prov. 12:11). Talking to the sluggard doesn't help him, nor does his conversation about his problem. "In all labor there is profit, but idle chatter [leads] only to poverty" (Prov. 14:23). When he goes to work, what will happen? "He who tills his land will have plenty of bread, but he who follows frivolity will have poverty enough!" (Prov. 28:19).

ENDNOTE

13. *Webster's New World Dictionary of the American Language, 2nd College Ed.* (Cleveland, Ohio: William Collins/World Publishing Co., Inc., 1974).

CHAPTER 25
Nothing Can Compare to Right-Believing

Lord, Solomon originated these proverbs;
The scribes of King Hezekiah copied them for us.
I know that You are glorified by concealing things;
It is the privilege of kings to search them out.
Just as the heaven is high and the earth is deep,
So the heart of a ruler is unknowable.

Lord, when impurities are removed from silver ore
The silver can make a beautiful vessel;
When the wicked are removed from public life,
The nation can live in righteousness.

Lord, I won't elevate myself over those around me
And I won't try to sit in a seat of honor;
Because it is better to be elevated to a higher seat
Than to be sent to the end of the line.

Lord, I won't rush to solve a dispute between neighbors,
Especially when I don't know all the facts;
Because I'll be embarrassed when one puts me to shame.
I'll discuss the problem with my neighbors
But I won't tell one what the other said to me;
Because if the first hears that I have told publicly
What he said to me privately,
Then I'll be embarrassed and my reputation will be ruined.

Lord, I know that apples of gold in a setting of silver
Is like an appropriate word spoken at the right time;
Just as a gold earring and necklace are appropriately worn,
So are the words of a counselor to a receptive ear.
Just as a cool breeze in the heat of harvest
So is one who always tells the truth,
Refreshing the heart of his employer.
Just as some of clouds and wind bring no rain,
So is the one who promises a gift
But disappoints because he never gives it.

Lord, I know that patience can win a stubborn leader,
And a soft answer can melt a hard heart.
I should only eat as much honey as I need when I find it
Because I'll throw up if I eat too much.
I should not visit my neighbor too much
Because he'll get sick of me and hate to see me come.

Lord, those who give false testimony against a neighbor
Hit them with a club, a sharp sword, or a piercing arrow.
When I rely on an untrustworthy person in a time of trouble,
It is like having a toothache or a crippled leg.

Lord, singing sad songs to people in trouble
Is like taking away their coat in cold weather.

Lord, when someone who hates me is hungry, I'll give him drink;
For then I'll heap hot coals (of shame) on his head
And You, Lord, will reward me.

Lord, just as a cold north wind brings rain,
So a backbiting tongue brings an angry stare.
It is better to live in a small corner of the roof
Than to live in a big house with a nagging wife.
Just as cold water quenches my thirst,
So good news from a distant source brings happiness.

Just as a muddy spring pollutes the drinking water,
So is a good person who compromises with the wicked.

Lord, I know it's not good to eat too much honey,
Nor is it wise to seek your own glory;
For both excesses will make you sick.

Lord, a great fortified city with breached walls
Is like a person without self-discipline.
Amen

CHAPTER 26

Watch Out for Fools and Scoundrels

Lord, I know that snow in the summer and rain at harvest
Are both out of place;
Just as giving honor to a fool.
I know that a bird struggling to fly will come home to roost,
So you will be punished with the curse you give
To someone who doesn't deserve it.

Lord, I know a whip will make a donkey obey
So correction is the only way to help a fool.
I'll not answer a fool according to his foolishness
Because I'll lower myself to his disgusting level;
But I'll answer a fool according to truth
So that he'll know he is not wise.
Letting a fool deliver a message for you
Is like asking for trouble and pain.
A wise saying in the mouth of a fool
Is about as good as a limp leg or useless arm;
A wise saying in the mouth of a fool
Does as much damage as grabbing a thorn bush with your hands.
Giving honor to a fool is like
Trying to shoot a gun without bullets.
A master craftsman can make a work of art,
But employing a fool breaks the laws of common sense.
A fool will always fool around about foolishness,
Just as a dog will return to his vomit;

Yet, there is more hope for a fool
Than for a conceited man who thinks he knows everything.

Lord, a lazy person makes excuses not to work
Saying there's a lion in the street.
Just as a door turns on its hinges,
So a lazy person continually turns over in bed;
He refuses to get up and go to work.
A lazy person puts his fork into his food,
But is too lazy to lift it to his mouth;
A lazy person has more excuses for what he does
Than the reasons of seven wise men.

Lord, if I get involved in a fight that's not my own
It's like grabbing a dog by its ears;
I'll get bitten.

Lord, those who deceive their neighbors, then say, "Just kidding,"
Are like ones shooting deadly arrows or firebrands.

Lord, I know when there's no wood, the fire goes out,
So when gossip stops, so does contention;
Just as coals are to a fire and burning wood makes heat,
So a quarreling person creates strife.

Lord, the lies of a slanderer are easily swallowed
But they make everyone sick to their stomach.
Just as silver covers a clay pot
So loving lips cover a hating heart;
Hateful people try to cover with pleasant words,
But they can't overcome their deceitful heart,
So I won't trust everyone who speaks pleasantly
Because they may be covering the abominations of their heart.
They may try to cover the hatred of their heart
But what's in the well comes up in the bucket;
So, eventually their hatred will come out.

139

Lord, those who dig a pit will eventually fall into it,
And what goes around will come around;
We will eventually suffer the evil we plan for others.

Lord, those who tell lies eventually hate their victims,
And a flattering tongue is a sugar-coated lie;
So I will tell the truth because I love You, Lord, and others.
Amen

CHARACTER SKETCH:
The Simple

"A prudent [man] foresees evil and hides himself, but the simple pass on and are punished" (Prov. 22:3). "The simple inherit folly, but the prudent are crowned with knowledge" (Prov. 14:18).

There is a difference between the simple and the fool. The simple is described as naïve or inexperienced in the ways of the world; being naïve he tends to believe any and everything. The Bible describes the simpleton as one who trusts everyone's advice. On the other hand, the fool is one who follows the wrong path, just as the simpleton, but the fool has a different attitude toward instruction. He despises truth, refuses wise instruction and does not want to follow common sense.

When it comes to a correct way of living, the issue is not correct knowledge or philosophy, rather the issue is the best way to live—the way God wants you to live. "The prudent considers well his steps" (Prov. 14:15). The simple man can think for himself, but is in danger of not doing so, but the fool who can think for himself refuses to do so. It is implied that the fool knows the better way, while the simpleton does not know the better way; but in spite of everything, the fool who knows the better way will not do it.

The wise person anticipates evil and mistakes and avoids them. "A prudent [man] foresees evil and hides himself, but the simple pass on and are punished" (Prov. 22:3) and Prov. 27:12 says, the fool chooses mischief and evil, while the simple blunders ahead full speed ending up with its consequences.

The naïve man doesn't think about consequences of his mistakes or the judgment of God on his sin. So, the Book of Proverbs is written to protect the simple, whereas Proverbs realizes that the fool will not listen to instructions, and therefore cannot be protected.

However, it's possible for the simple to become a fool. One does not stay naïve forever because consequences are a teacher. When you make mistakes they hurt, and you should learn from them, but the simpleton grows up in his experiences and grows away from God's principles. As a result, his obvious stupidity becomes insipid rebellion.

The wise are committed to learning wisdom, "Wisdom [is] in the sight of him who has understanding, but the eyes of a fool [are] on the ends of the earth" (Prov. 17:24). By staying focused on God's plan, the wise become even wiser, and their life becomes better.

Next, the wise learn from their experiences, "Rebuke is more effective for a wise [man] than a hundred blows on a fool" (Prov. 17:10), and "Though you grind a fool in a mortar with a pestle along with crushed grain, [yet] his foolishness will not depart from him" (Prov. 27:22). These proverbs are saying that the fool resists instruction from the voice of experience, but the wise man learns from them.

When the simple becomes a fool, he remains in his foolish condition because his appetite for rebellion against God's principles is greater than his desire to avoid the consequences of life. What is a fool like? "As a dog returns to his own vomit, [so] a fool repeats his folly" (Prov. 26:11).

1. The simple person was not morally wrong, but simply had not grown. Everyone is young at one time, and all must learn the lessons of life. So, we all begin at the starting line, no one is born with intelligence, nor are they better than anyone else.

2. The simple person cannot stay in that state, just as a baby cannot remain uneducated. Every baby must be taught something, whether to obey or disobey, whether to take care of itself or to depend on others. So the simple will be faced with a choice of following God or willfully rebelling against Him.

3. The simple person does not naturally grow out of being simple. Natural growth does not produce a wise person,

rather, the wise person must choose to learn and the parents of children must attempt to teach their children the correct choices in life (Prov. 1:10,15,22-23).

4. The simple person is in a dangerous position because the simple lacks wisdom, therefore he must learn knowledge and wise living (Prov. 1:4) and understanding (Prov. 9:4,16), and common sense (7:7), or he will suffer the consequences of wrong choices or no choices.

The simple are inclined toward rebellion, not toward God's principles. It's only natural for the simple to love his simplicity. "How long, you simple ones, will you love simplicity?" (Prov. 1:22). But if they stay in that condition, it will eventually destroy them. "For the turning away of the simple will slay them, and the complacency of fools will destroy them" (Prov. 1:32). The rebel often tries to get the simple to rebel with him. Because the young son is often simple, the book of Proverbs directs the young son how to be wise. "My son, keep my words, and treasure my commands within you. Keep my commands and live, and my law as the apple of your eye" (Prov. 7:1,2).

The fool who rebels against God will try to get the simpleton to rebel with him. Why is this? Because "misery loves company" and those who feel good about doing the wrong thing, want to get everyone else to feel what they feel.

And also, the trollop is after the simpleton. She calls to him, trying to get him into her bed (Prov. 7:6-26; 9:13-18).

The simple must make a choice to turn from the trollop and the fool, reject their wicked ways, and instead pursue wisdom (Prov. 1:23; 2:1-11; 3:1-26; 4:1-27).

5. The simple did not fall to the trollop because he was soulful. While the observer was sitting at his window watching the simpleton in the streets, he saw certain things. The simple fell to the woman because he was at the wrong place where she was located (Prov. 7:7,8). The trollop does not "stalk her prey," but she waits for the simple to come to her (Prov. 7:7,8,9,10). The simple was out wandering the streets at night, rather than in his home sleeping, or doing what he was supposed to do (Prov. 7:8). The simple was outwardly intrigued by the trollop and wanted to learn more about her. She was very willing to tell him all about herself (7:13-20). It wasn't as though he planned to sin

with her, he was wrongly satisfying his curiosity. Like many young people, he wanted to see how closely he could walk to the edge without falling off.

6. The simple was not deceived, but was seduced. Notice that when she approaches the simple, she kisses him (Prov. 7:13) and tells him all the pleasures they can enjoy together. No matter how simple this young man, he knew what she was suggesting. And for whatever reasons he was in her neighborhood, he knew what would happen. He should have been running for his spiritual life instead of playing with fire.

Proverbs

CHAPTER 27
Right-Believing Leads to Good Relationships

Lord, I'll not boast what I'll do tomorrow
For I don't know what a future day will bring.
I'll let another talk about my accomplishments
Because no one will believe my boasting;
I'll let an objective observer do it.
Stones are heavy to pick up, so is sand;
But a fool's anger outweighs them both.

Lord, I know that wrath is cruel, and anger is outrageous
But the revenge of a jealous person is greater than both.
I would rather have open rebuke to become wise
And know where I stand with a person,
Than have hidden love that I never experience,
And not realize the love that was mine.
I would rather have wounds from a friend,
Than deceitful kisses from an enemy.

Lord, when I'm full I have no taste for honey;
But when I'm hungry, anything bitter tastes sweet.

Lord, a man who foolishly strays from his home
Is like a bird that abandons his protective nest.

Lord, just as perfume and sweet-smelling things make us happy
So does good advice from the heart of a friend.

145

Lord, I'll not abandon a loyal friend
Who is also a life-long friend of my father;
I'll not go for help to a relative who is far away
Rather, I'll go to a friend who is near.
I want to become wise to make my father glad,
Then I won't need my father to answer my critics.
I want to be wise to avoid trouble when it comes;
Fools don't think about the future and pay the price.

Lord, I'll not sign a note for a stranger
So they can't take the coat off my back;
They'll probably seize another man's clothing,
To pay the debts he incurred because of his sin.

Lord, I'll not yell a blessing to my neighbor before dawn,
For I'll waken him and he will curse me.

Lord, a nagging wife that keeps fussing
Is like dripping water on a rainy day;
It will only irritate and anger.
The one who can restrain the negative wife
Can also restrain the wind;
Of course neither can be done.

Lord, just as iron is used to sharpen a knife,
So I can sharpen the outlook of my friend.
Those who carefully look after the fig tree
Get to enjoy its fruit.
Those who do what their boss wants done,
Will be honored and promoted.
Just as I can see my image reflected in water,
So others can see my heart by looking at my face.

Lord, the greed that motivates my heart to want many things,
Is like hell and the grave;
Neither are ever satisfied.

Just as the fire tests silver, and the crucible tests gold,
So my character will be tested by its reaction to praise.

Lord, I can grind a fool in the mill with a grinder
Just as grain is crushed to powder;
Yet his foolishness will remain.

Lord, I'll take care of the health of my flocks
And I'll pay attention to the number in my herds;
Because a man's riches are eventually lost,
And a business won't stay in the family forever.
So, when the hay has been mown for winter feeding
And the vegetables have been gathered from the garden,
The wool of my lambs will provide clothing;
There will be enough goats' milk for all to drink
And I can sell my extra goats for a profit.
Then I can buy enough food to get my family through the winter
And have enough to give a bonus to my employees.
Amen

Proverbs

CHAPTER 28

Use Common Sense When Being Religious

Lord, the wicked have terror in their hearts
Because they have no confidence in life;
The righteous have the self-confidence of a lion
Because they know You, they feel sure of themselves.
Because we live in a world of sin,
We need many rulers to make people do right;
But there is coming a ruler—a man of understanding;
His Kingdom will rule all—it will endure.

Lord, when I see one poor man oppressing another poor man,
It's like a rain storm that washes away all food;
For the poor don't realize they need each other to survive.
Those who abandon their principles end up loving sin,
But those who obey Your principles oppose them who love sin;
Evil people don't understand absolute truth and judgment
But they who seek to please You, understand all things.

Lord, it's better for me to tell the truth and end up poor
Than it is to get rich by living a lie;
I'll be Your wise child who obeys Your truth
Because those who hang out with fools disappoint their father.

Lord, those who get rich by charging too much
Create wealth for someone else to give it to the poor.
Those who refuse to obey Your principles
Will not get their prayers answered.

Those who tempt the righteous to break Your law
Shall suffer the punishment he plans for them;
But the upright who does not give into temptation
Will get the good things You have for him.

Lord, the rich man believes everything he does is all right,
But the wise poor man can see through his deceit.
When the good man wins, everyone rejoices
But no one wants to see a wicked man win.
Those who hide their sin, will not get away with it
But You accept those who confess and repent;
Those who fear and obey You are happy
But those who harden their hearts will have a hard life.

Lord, a hungry roaring lion and prowling bear
Are like a wicked leader who eats up the poor;
A rising leader without wisdom is a cruel oppressor
But leaders who hate greed shall stay in office.

Lord, the one who kills another deserves to die;
Don't let anyone get him off the hook.
Those who obey Your principles shall be saved;
Those who reject Your ways will not live long.

Lord, those who work hard at their job will have food to eat
But those who frolic with lazy people will be poor;
Those trustworthy workers will receive bonuses and raises
But those who cut corners will be demoted or fired.

Lord, it's wrong to be partial to any person
Because all people are of one blood and
Were created in Your image.

Lord, the greedy person will sell his soul for money
Not knowing his insatiable appetite

149

Will ultimately choke him to death;
But a starving man will steal for bread.

Lord, if I correct my brother to help him
I'll get more gratitude
Than if I flatter his sin and disobedience.

Lord, those who steal from their parents saying,
"I deserve it because I'm their child,"
Are a brother to satan.

Lord, those who grasp after attention
Create strife and anger in those around him;
But those who obey Your principles
Will prosper and get the right kind of attention.
Those who trust in themselves are fools,
But the ones living right will prosper.
Those who give to the poor will not lack anything,
But those who turn their backs will be cursed by them.
When the wicked are in power,
Good people hide because they are punished;
But when the wicked are kicked out of office,
Everyone flourishes.
Amen

The King

"Mercy and truth preserve the king, and by lovingkindness he upholds his throne" (Prov. 20:28). "The king's heart [is] in the hand of the Lord, [Like] the rivers of water; He turns it wherever He wishes" (Prov. 21:1). "By me (wisdom) kings reign" (Prov. 8:15). "Righteous lips [are] the delight of kings, and they love him who speaks [what is] right" (Prov. 16:13).

According to the Book of Proverbs, the wise king (living by principles) will have a good reign. The same with a godly government, if it is administered by a godly king. However, the principles of management or administration are applied to all who are leaders of others; therefore, the presidents of colleges, business owners and those who manage programs for the government.

The administrator must rule by right principles. When the king rules by right principles, "Righteousness exalts a nation, But sin [is] a reproach to [any] people" (Prov. 14:34), and "When a wicked [man] rules, the people groan" (Prov. 29:2).

Since God instituted government, He expects governmental leaders to rule by right principles. As a result, the nation will be righteous.

God expects the king to speak the truth, uphold the truth, and govern by truth. "Mercy and truth preserve the king, and by lovingkindness he upholds his throne" (Prov. 20:28). Also, "the king who judges the poor with truth, His throne will be established forever" (Prov. 29:14). But the opposite is also true. "A ruler who lacks understanding [is] a great oppressor" (Prov. 28:16).

God puts kings in their position. When the people are good, God usually gives them a good king. But when they do evil, God allows an evil king to rule over them. "The king's heart [is] in the hand of the Lord, [Like] the rivers of water; He turns it wherever He wishes" (Prov. 21:1). God puts a king or business administrator in a position to manage by right principles. "By me (wisdom) kings reign" (Prov. 8:15).

A king must be fair and impartial. A bad king will not be fair to all people. "A wicked [man] accepts a bribe behind the back to pervert the ways of justice" (Prov. 17:23). So, "[It is] not good to show partiality to the wicked, [or] to overthrow the righteous in judgment" (Prov. 18:5). King Lemuel decreed that it is the duty of a king to be fair and not "pervert the justice of all the afflicted" (Prov. 31:5). Because drunkenness destroys the understanding of a leader, King Lemuel declared, "[It is] not for kings to drink wine, nor for princes intoxicating drink; lest they drink and forget the law, and pervert the justice of all the afflicted" (Prov. 31:4,5).

A king must not abuse his power. Many of the Old Testament kings abused the power that was given them by God, such as Ahab, Manassas, etc. Proverbs teaches, "A ruler who lacks understanding [is] a great oppressor, [but] he who hates covetousness will prolong [his] days" (Prov. 28:16). What is a king to do? "Open your mouth for the speechless, in the cause of all [who are] appointed to die. Open your mouth, judge righteously, and plead the cause of the poor and needy" (Prov. 31:8,9). The king must punish evil doers and protect the innocent from crime.

Proverbs says that the king "sits on the throne of judgment" (Prov. 20:8), they must make good decisions based on correct principles. The king is not supposed to accept bribes from the wicked, nor to give evil people any leniency. "Take away the wicked from before the king, and his throne will be established in righteousness" (Prov. 25:5). No one should enjoy seeing another man suffer, but it is the duty of a king to punish the wicked and protect the righteous. The king must uphold the laws which are "right principles." The Book of Proverbs teaches, "When the scoffer is punished, the simple is made wise" (Prov. 21:11).

So the king should protect those who are wise enough to do the right thing, "The king's favor [is] toward a wise servant, but his wrath [is against] him who causes shame" (Prov. 14:35). "Righteous lips [are] the delight of kings, and they love him who speaks [what is] right" (Prov. 16:13). Therefore, a king should listen to those who speak right and follow their counsel.

Who should be a counselor to the king? "He who loves purity of heart [and has] grace on his lips, The king [will be] his friend" (Prov. 22:11).

The king should be obeyed. Because the king rules in the place of God, Proverbs teaches, "My son, fear the Lord and the king; do not associate with those given to change; for their calamity will rise suddenly, and who knows the ruin those two can bring?" (Prov. 24:21,22).

The king should be a servant-leader. While the Book of Proverbs was written to teach Solomon how to rule the people, he failed to follow its advice. At times he had a heavy hand on his people (1 Kings 12:4). When Solomon's son Rehoboam came to the throne, he was advised, "If you will be a servant to these people today, and serve them, and answer them, and speak good words to them, then they will be your servants forever" (I Kings 12:7). But Rehoboam had not learned to be a servant-leader, he abused the people. As a result, they rebelled and his kingdom was split in half.

Conclusion

Proverbs teaches that the king (or administrator) must have wisdom, i.e., right-believing that leads to right-living. When the king rules the people by righteousness, the nation prospers. When the king rules by evil principles, the people suffer.

CHAPTER 29
Right-Believing Will Make You a Good Citizen

Lord, those who harden their will after being rebuked
Will be suddenly broken.
When the righteous are our leaders
Everyone rejoices because they do right;
But when the wicked are over us,
Everyone moans because evil flourishes.

Lord, when I seek to think the right way,
I make my father glad;
But those who visit a prostitute
Waste their money and their life.
Rulers gives us a stable nation when they do right,
But rulers that take bribes destroy a people.
Those who try to get ahead by flattery
Spread a trap for their feet.
The crimes of an evil man will eventually catch him,
But the righteous sing and dance
because they have a clean conscience.

Lord, the righteous are always concerned about the poor;
But the wicked are selfish people,
They don't care about anyone but themselves.
A negative critic gets everyone mad,
But the words of the wise have a calming effect.

When a wise man argues with a fool,
He only gets scorn, and angry replies.

Those who want to kill, hate those who obey God's principles
And will attempt to do away with them.
The fool rattles on about everything he doesn't like,
But a wise person holds his tongue, and thinks through the situation.
Those leaders who listen and believe lies
Have counselors around them who are wicked.

Lord, You have given a conscience of right and wrong
To the poor and the oppressor;
When the leader honestly trusts the poor,
He will be in office a long time.

Lord, You've given us means to correct our children,
But the child left to himself will disgrace his parents;
So discipline your child and he will make you happy;
Yes, he will do what you expect him to do.

Lord, when I don't have divine direction in my life,
I'll shrivel and die spiritually;
But I'm happy when I obey Your law.

Lord, it's hard to discipline workers with words;
They may understand, but they won't obey.
Those people who have something to say about everything
Have as much hope as a fool.
If I pamper a child from youth,
He will be ungrateful when he grows up.
Angry people stir up strife and bitterness;
People with uncontrollable tempers commit crimes.

Lord, I will be brought low if I am proud,
But I will be honored when I humble myself.

Lord, he who partners with a thief, hates himself;
When he hears people curse the thief
He doesn't say anything.

Lord, the fear of man brings a snare
But those who put their trust in You will be safe;
Many seek the leaders' favor
But they get justice from You, Lord.

Lord, the wicked man is always against the righteous person,
And the righteous person is detested by the wicked.
Amen

Proverbs

CHAPTER 30
The Knowledge God Would Have You Know

Lord, Solomon received a message from You
To give to Ithiel and Ucal.

Lord, the one who is more boorish than others
Is too ignorant to seek to understand God;
He lacks human understanding and wisdom.
He doesn't have enough common sense
To know You, the Holy One.

Lord, You are the only One who has access
To both Heaven and earth.
You hold the wind in Your cupped hands;
You wrap up the oceans in Your cloak.
You created the whole earth
From one end to the other.
Only You know Your name,
And Your Son's name.

Lord, every word that You speak is pure;
You protect those who take refuge in You.
If I add anything to Your words,
You will rebuke me
And I'll be made to be a liar.

Lord, I have asked two things from You
To help me all my life.

158

Don't let me tell a lie or misrepresent the truth,
And give me neither poverty nor riches;
Just give me the food I need each day.
If I have too much money, I may deny You
And say, "Who is the Lord?"
If I am too poor, I might steal
And tarnish Your name, O Lord.

Lord, I will never criticize a person to his employer
Because he will slander me for my interference.
I know there are those who curse their fathers
And don't bless their mothers.
These people justify their actions
And think they never do anything wrong;
They are haughty and stupid.

Lord, there are critics whose teeth are sharp like razors;
Their tongues are like daggers.
They eat up everyone with their sarcasm
And criticize those who need the most help.

Lord, the leech sucks the life out of things,
Always crying more! More! More!
There are three things—no, there are four
That want more and are never satisfied.
The grave,
A barren womb,
The dusty desert,
A blazing fire.

Lord, the eye that mocks his father,
And criticizes the request of his mother,
Will be pecked out by the birds;
And that one will be judged for his rebellion.

Lord, there are three things that are wonderful.
When I add a fourth, I am amazed:

The way an eagle floats in the sky,
The way a snake slithers on a rock,
The way a ship glides under the wind,
The way of a man with a woman.

Lord, it seems an unfaithful wife excuses herself;
She wipes her mouth saying, "I did nothing wrong."

Lord, three things make the earth quake,
Add a fourth thing and everything trembles:
A slave who becomes a king,
A fool who gets rich,
A complaining woman who finally gets a husband,
A servant girl who takes the place of her mistress.

Lord, four things on the earth are very small,
But they are wise:
Ants who are not mighty but they store food for the winter,
Little badgers who make their home in the holes of the rocks,
Locusts that have no leader but they march in ranks,
Spiders that are tiny enough to get into the king's palace.

Lord, three things march stately with dignity;
No, add a fourth that also strides:
The lion that turns aside for none,
The swiftest greyhound that can't be caught,
The stubborn billy goat that won't back down,
The king leading his army.

Lord, I hope all boorish fools
Are smart enough to keep quiet
So people won't see their stupid ways.
Just as churning milk produces butter,
And pressure on the nose produces blood,
So the pressure of anger produces strife.
Amen

CHARACTER SKETCH:

A Wife Worth More Than Rubies

"Who can find a virtuous wife? For her worth [is] far above rubies. The heart of her husband safely trusts her; so he will have no lack of gain. She does him good and not evil all the days of her life" (Prov. 31:10-12).

Proverbs describes the wife as a "virtuous woman" and gives you a look at her actions, character, and then finally her rewards.

1. *She is a godly woman.* The most identifiable thing about her is the concluding statement, "But a woman [who] fears the Lord, she shall be praised" (Prov. 31:30). She shall be praised not for her outward beauty or charm, but her inner walk with God. She has moral character. A person of character is described as doing the right thing in the right way. And she is described as "an excellent wife" (Prov. 31:10 NAS) rather than being clothed in expensive garments, she is clothed with strength and dignity (Prov. 31:25). Because this woman is so virtuous and hard to find, one must search for her (Prov. 31:10).

2. *She is worthy of her family's trust.* While the husband is out working, he does not have to worry about the wife. "The heart of her husband safely trusts her" (Prov. 31:11). He not only knows that he can trust her character to be faithful

to him, he also can trust her hard-working ability to take care of the house, the children, and become a producer of moral character in other people.

3. *She works conscientiously.* Whereas the Proverbs deride the sluggard repeatedly, it describes the virtuous woman as one who works with her hands (Prov. 31:13). She gets up early (Prov. 31:15) and goes to sleep late (Prov. 31:18). She is making long-range plans (Prov. 31:21, 25) and she doesn't sit around with idle time watching soap operas or taking long naps (Prov. 31:27). She is a relative who buys a field (Prov 31:16); she works in the vineyard (Prov. 31:16) and makes sure her husband and children are well-clothed (Prov. 31:12), and she herself is well-clothed (Prov. 31:22).

4. *She has a humanitarian spirit.* She is concerned about the needy, the poor and she gives to their needs (Prov. 31:20).

5. *She is the family shopper.* According to Proverbs she looks after cloth, and gets food from afar (Prov. 31:14).

6. *She is a good household manager.* This means the virtuous woman is able to feed the entire family and administer the things that she has. She gets up early in the morning to prepare breakfast, and gives tasks to everyone in the household (Prov. 31:15).

7. *She supervises long-range investments.* Did you see the fact that "she considers a field and buys it; from her profits she plants a vineyard" (Prov. 31:16). Also, "She makes linen garments and sells [them,] and supplies sashes for the merchants" (Prov. 34:24). Rather than being a wife who sits around waiting for her husband to give her money, she uses well what she has and adds to the family checkbook.

8. *She is not a gossiper but speaks words of encouragement.* Whether speaking to her husband, children or others, "She opens her mouth with wisdom, and on her tongue [is] the law of kindness" (Prov. 31:26).

9. *She supports her husband.* This is not a woman who takes glory to herself, or becomes the spokesperson in the local church while her husband stands around with the men in the back of the church. Rather, "Her husband is known in the gates, when he sits among the elders of the land" (Prov. 31:23). By lifting up her husband, he in turn lifts her up.

Proverbs

CHAPTER 31
What Is a Godly Woman?

Lord, I will live by the preaching of Solomon
The message that was given him by his mother, Bathsheba.
It is the biggest vow that could be asked
By a mother of her son,
And I promise to keep this pledge.
I will not give my strength to whorish women,
To an adulterous life that would destroy me.
I will not seek pleasure in strong drink, nor will I ever taste liquor;
Because drinking will distort my understanding of Your law
And drunkenness will make me forget my duties.
Liquor will not give happiness, but brings misery;
And those who are given to strong drink will be destroyed.
They drink to forget their emptiness
And forget about all their problems.

Lord, I will speak for those who don't know what to say;
I will give Your Word to those who are perishing.
I will always do the right thing;
I will open my heart to the needs of the poor.

Prayer for Men (31:10-31)

Lord, I will search for a virtuous woman;
I know she is worth far more than rubies.
My heart will safely trust in such a woman,
And I will find happiness with her.

A virtuous woman will do me good,
And not evil all the days of her life.
She will get the finest cloth for her clothes,
And dress appropriately at all times.
She goes everywhere that is necessary
To get the best food for our family.
She gets up early to prepare food
So our family will have nourishing meals.
She has the business savvy to purchase a field
And get it planted so our family will have extra food.
She has strength to get everything done,
And more strength to stand for the right.
She knows that her task in life is good,
And she continually works at it.
She is smart enough to do every task in the home,
And she has the determination to get them done.
She has a humanitarian heart for the needy,
And gives money to help them.
She prepares for all types of weather;
All in our home are comfortably clothed.

Her outward clothes are as beautiful
As her inward loveliness and godliness.
I will have a good reputation in the community because of her,
And I will use my influence for that which is right.

She is industrious with her time,
And is able to earn extra income.
She knows the principles of wisdom,
And is able to kindly explain Your law.
She makes sure everyone in our household
Lives by the principles of wisdom.

Her children quickly credit her for their success,
And I wouldn't be prosperous without her.
There are many good women in the world,

But the virtuous woman You gave me exceeds them all.
Beauty deceives some women, and compliments sidetrack others;
But she is a woman who puts her trust in You,
And is worthy of all the compliments she gets.
She deserves all the things she works for,
And her accomplishments are her praise.

Prayer for Women (31:10-31)

Lord, I want to be a virtuous woman
Whose price is worth more than rubies.
I want my husband to trust me in his heart,
And find happiness in me.
I want to do good things for my husband,
And not tempt him to deny his faith.
I determine to dress appropriately at all times
In the best available clothes I have.
I will do whatever is necessary
To get the appropriate food for my family.
I will get up early to prepare food
So my family will have nourishing meals.
I will use the ability You gave me
To buy a field and plant food for my family.

Lord, give me strength to get everything done,
And moral strength to stand for the right.
I know my task in life is good;
Help me do the best job possible.

Lord, give me wisdom to do everything for my home,
And the self-discipline to get it done.
Give me a compassionate heart for the needy;
I will give money to help them.
I will prepare for all types of weather,
And make sure that all of my family are comfortably clothed.

Lord, I want my outward clothes
To reflect the inward beauty that You've given me.
I want my husband to have a good reputation
In the community in which we live.

Lord, help me to use all my time wisely,
So I can earn extra income for the family.
Help me think properly what leads to success;
I want to make sure everyone in my household
lives by Your principles.
I want my children to appreciate my godly influence,
And my husband to tell others how I've helped him.

Lord, there are many good women in the world,
But I want to be the virtuous woman You described.
I know outward beauty can deceive me
And compliments can sidetrack me.
I want the inward beauty that comes
Because I put my trust in You.
May my compliments come from the things I've accomplished,
And may my praise be the family I've raised.
Amen

PRAYING
ECCLESIASTES
To Avoid Trouble and Sin

INTRODUCTION

The word *ecclesiastes* is the Latin title of this book. The Hebrews called the book, "Qoheleth", i.e., the preacher. The Hebrew term *qoheleth* occurs only in Ecclesiastes, nowhere else in the Old Testament, and comes from *qohel*, which Martin Luther translated, *der prediger*, which means *the preacher*. Hence, the writer of the book is the preacher.

The preacher is not identified as Solomon, the book is introduced, "The words of the preacher, the son of David, the king in Jerusalem" (Eccles. 1:1 KJV). Since Solomon was the only son of David who was king of Israel, there can be no doubt that he was the author. Later he says, "I, the preacher (*qoheleth*), was king over Israel in Jerusalem" (Eccles. 1:12).

Also, the Hebrew order of books had them appear in the order of Proverbs, Ecclesiastes, and Canticles (Song of Solomon), suggesting that Solomon wrote the book of Ecclesiastes because it has been definitely proven that he wrote the books before and after.

Also, Solomon was the founder of the "Wisdom Movement" (1 Kings 4:27-32), so that as the preacher, Solomon would be extremely qualified to pass judgment on the true value of wisdom and riches, as opposed to the opinions of modern man concerning vanity, wealth, and pursuit of physical pleasure, i.e., eat, drink, and be merry. And lest any of the critics think otherwise, the discovery of Hebrew fragments of Ecclesiastes at Qumran (the Dead Sea scrolls) indicate that a copy of this book was in circulation extremely early, i.e., before the time of

Christ (*Tmuilendurg, Bulletin of the American Schools of Oriental Research,* 135, 1954, pp. 20-28).

When Ecclesiastes Was Written

According to Jewish tradition, Solomon wrote the *Song of Songs*, i.e., *The Song of Solomon*, with its passionate emphasis on love when he was a young man. It tells the story of his meeting the Shulamite, falling in love with her, and first marrying her after he became king of Israel. Solomon's second book is Proverbs that emphasizes practical wisdom. Since Solomon built his kingdom on wisdom and through good leadership principles, he became more powerful; he chronicled these principles in Proverbs. Inasmuch as the Book of Proverbs exhorts a young man to get knowledge so he can gain wisdom, today's title might be *Believing Right for Successful Living.* The Hebrew tradition says the third book, Ecclesiastes, was written by Solomon in his old age after the successes and failures of many marriages, the lack of contentment with luxury, and the boredom of power and authority. It is then when he asks, "What profit has a man from all his labor in which he toils under the sun?" (Eccles. 1:3). He concludes money, luxury, and sexual exploits are all "vanity of vanities," i.e., meaningless and pointless.

Negative Perspective

Through the years, many people have been perplexed at the negative attitudes of Ecclesiastes. This is the preacher's attempt to show the futility of life lived apart from God's principles. The preacher begins, "vanity of vanities" (Eccles. 1:2) which is translated in this volume as "life is meaningless and purposeless." Then the preacher asks the question, "What profit has a man from all his labor in which he toils under the sun?" (Eccles. 1:3). The word "profit" is the Hebrew word *yithron*, a word unique to Ecclesiastes drawn from the business world. It means a financial profit, gain, superiority, or preeminence. What can man gain from a fallen world? This is the same question the Lord Jesus asked, "For what will it profit a man if he gains the whole world, and loses his own soul?" (Mark 8:36). If a man knows all the wisdom of the world, but doesn't know God, and he experiences all of the pleasures of this world, but doesn't put God first, and he has all the wealth and luxuries, would life be worthwhile apart from God?

The phrase, "vanity of vanities," from the Hebrew *hebel*, is one of the preacher's favorite phrases, used 35 times in this book. It means, vapor or a breath. The preacher is saying that life without God is about as significant as a breeze that passed by a few minutes ago. In a world of millions of breezes, what meaning or purpose does any one of them have? What difference can you make and how different can you live? In this book, "vanity of vanities" is translated "worthless and meaningless."

Even though some people think the preacher is teaching words that are contrary to Scripture, this is not the truth. He is *describing* the emptiness of life apart from God, not *prescribing* vanity as a way of life.

Over the years, many cults and false religions have appealed to various passages in Ecclesiastes to prove their variant doctrines, or immoral lifestyles. But living the sins in Ecclesiastes is not God's way to live. Rather the reader is told about an immoral life to persuade him not to live this way.

When you read Ecclesiastes, distinguish between the "goad" passages, and "nail" passages. The preacher makes a difference between them, "The words of the wise are like goads, and the words of scholars are like well-driven nails, given by one Shepherd" (Eccles. 12:11). The goads are the negative principles found in Ecclesiastes. He does not mean that these principles should be followed, but rather the reader should reject them because they will lead to a life of vanity.

So, when reading the book of Ecclesiastes, bring the whole Scriptural perspective to its pages. The *goad* passages are negative, which are to be avoided (Eccles. 1:2-18; 2:1-11; 3:12-13; 4:1-3, 13-16; 5:1-7; 6:1-12). The seven "nail" passages give positive exhortations to follow, (Eccles. 3:1-11,14-21; 7:1-29; 8:1-9; 9:18; 10:1-20; 11:1-7; 12:7).

The preacher discovers the goads by studying the heart of man, and the negative consequences they bring. What do goads produce in the reader? Guilt, fear, failure, frustration, and remorseful memories. But the nails are those positive things that are found in the revelation of God, i.e., what He wants us to think and do. The nails produce stability, inner peace, purpose, and a reason for living.

The Book of Ecclesiastes is a summary of Solomon's failures, disappointment and struggles. He encountered these as he built his kingdom, married his many wives, and accumulated his wealth. However, none of these brought him happiness.

The Book of Ecclesiastes arrives at a fundamental conclusion about life. First, deep contentment and lasting purpose in life are found in obedience to God (Eccles. 2:24-26; 3:22; 5:18-20). Second, the fundamental duty of man is to reverentially trust God by observing the principles that lead to wisdom and success (Eccles. 12:13). Ecclesiastes is a remorseful autobiography of a wise man who didn't apply his life to what he knew to do.

Solomon's Wisdom

As a young man, Solomon was called upon by God to make a life-choice, and he prayed rightly for wisdom rather than for wealth or long life, or victory over his enemies. As a result, Solomon was given "a wise and understanding heart" (1 Kings 3:9-13). But, with his wise heart eventually came riches, honor, and leisure. Solomon understood the principles of right-believing and right-living. Solomon is the founder of the "Wisdom Movement" (Eccles. 13:1; 14:1).

The fundamental fault of Solomon was not heeding principles he wrote concerning the "strange woman." While this strange woman was a trollop who lusted after sexual pleasure, the "strange woman" was also a woman who was a stranger to the covenant relationship to Jehovah. She was not a Hebrew, hence not a believer. So Solomon's problem was not just a "sex problem" of committing adultery, it was a spiritual problem of compromising with a mixed marriage, "But King Solomon loved many foreign women" (1 Kings 11:1).

As a result, Solomon put the love of women and the satisfying of the flesh above the wisdom that he originally wrote and pursued in the book of Proverbs (1 Kings 11:4-8). And what is the fruit of Solomon's life? Rather than being known for his wisdom and establishing the kingdom of his father David, Solomon was responsible for the division of the kingdom. Solomon's son Rehoboam was born of "Naamah, the Ammonitess" (1 Kings 14:21-31). Because Solomon married foreign women in defiance of the instructions of God, and sought sexual satisfaction with them, he rebelled against divine instruction, and breached the divine covenant. No wonder his son, Rehoboam, split the kingdom and brought ruin upon the people of God.

Ecclesiastes

CHAPTER 1

To Realize the Vanity of a Life Without Purpose

Lord, I want to hear the prophetic words of Solomon,
The son of David, the king in Jerusalem.
Vanity of vanities concludes Solomon.
Life seems pointless and meaningless;
Nothing is worth our work, and nothing counts.

Lord, what can I get for all my work and concern
For just toiling in the hot sun?
What will I get for all my work on Earth
If life is empty and nothing matters?

Lord, I know that generations come, and generations go,
But everything remains the same on Earth.
The sun comes up each morning and sets each evening
No matter what I do on this earth;
The sun speeds across the heavens at the same rate.
The hot wind blows from the south,
Then a cold wind whistles in from the north.
The wind continues to blow in every direction,
Then it starts the same cycle again.

Lord, all the rivers flow to the sea;
Why doesn't the sea fill and overflow?

Yet, everywhere I look, the rivers continue flowing;
They never empty the place from which they begin.

Lord, life seems pointless and meaningless;
I seem to accomplish little for all I do.
The eye never sees what is seeable,
And the ear never hears what is hearable.
What has happened in the past will happen in the future;
What was accomplished before will be accomplished again,
And under the sun, there is nothing new.

Lord, can anyone ever say, "This is new?"
No! It existed in the past long ago.
No one cares about the people who used to live
And those in the future will not be remembered,
Just as we who live today will be forgotten.

The preacher says there is no new thing under the sun (Eccles. 1:9). This is not a pronouncement that there will be no new inventions, but the laws of gravity that control the earth don't change, neither does the human nature change. Solomon says life has a monotonous sameness. Even though new things are invented, life is still the same. People have the same dreary response to life. Everyone continues to ask "Why am I living?" Because the man who doesn't know God has limited knowledge and doesn't understand why he is here, nothing is new to him.

When you try to achieve earthly values, what do you achieve? What value is earthly achievement compared to knowing God and serving Him? Without God we are basically a helpless victim of humanity's brutal actions. When God is left out of our life, nothing worthwhile is left.

Lord, I know that You gave wisdom to Solomon, King of Israel;
He became the wisest man on Earth.
He applied his wisdom to investigate everything on Earth,
Yet Solomon's wisdom made him a cynic
Because he did not make You the center of all inquiry.
After seeing everything under the sun,
Solomon felt everything was pointless and meaningless.

He said, "What is crooked can't be made straight,
And you can't count what you don't have."
Solomon boasted he had more knowledge than anyone before him,
Yet when he tried to apply his knowledge to life
He was blown about by every wind and thought.
In himself, Solomon felt stupid and foolish.
Solomon concluded that we are frustrated when we know too much,
And more wisdom brings more frustration.
Amen

Ecclesiastes

CHAPTER 2
To Realize the Purpose in Work

Lord, Solomon tried to find life's meaning
with pleasures and good things,
But pleasure is not the purpose of life;
It is pointlessly self-serving.
Solomon tried to find life's meaning through wine
and bodily fulfillment,
But the right-believing person realizes that's foolishness.
Solomon tried to find the best thing in life to do,
With the short period of time he had to live.
Solomon worked hard and built great palaces,
Then he surrounded them with beautiful parks,
Where he planted all kinds of trees
And he dug exquisite pools to water the greenery.
And Solomon looked at all his property and said,
"Possessions are pointless and meaningless,
Nothing is worth my work, and nothing counts."

Lord, Solomon acquired male and female servants
To do all his work for him;
He enjoyed a life of ease.
He had huge herds of cattle and flocks of sheep,
He had more than any before him.
He employed male and female singers to entertain him,
And delighted himself with sexual experiences.
He had great wealth and was more powerful than any before him,
And he tried to retain the wisdom You gave him.

He denied his greed nothing that he wanted,
And withheld no fantasy from his experience.
Because Solomon worked hard to gain all he had,
He felt he deserved every experience he had;
Yet Solomon realized every advantage was meaningless
For he found no satisfaction in all he had.
He said, "What do I get for all my work and concern?"
Life is empty and nothing matters.

Lord, then Solomon re-examined the path of wise right-thinking.
He saw that no one could do
Anything but what had already been done.

Lord, Solomon said that wisdom is more useful than foolishness,
Just as light is more useful than darkness.
Lord, I know the right-thinking man sees where he walks,
But the fool walks in darkness;
Yet both the wise and fool eventually die.

Lord, when I'm wise the same thing will happen to me
That will happen to fools when they die.
So why should I live wisely?
Both the wise and the fool will be forgotten after they die;
Both the wise and the fool eventually die.

They will forget everything in the future
that happened in the past;
So why should I try?
Or why should I care?

Solomon came to hate his life
Because everything he did was pointless and meaningless;
Nothing was worth his work, and nothing counts.

Solomon is saying that building a good reputation is not a satisfying purpose to life. While a good reputation gets you many things and can be satisfying, there is a better answer than being well known. It's having a good relationship with God.

Lord, Solomon hated all the things he did in life,
Because he'd have to leave them to someone after him.
Who knows if the one who gets my inheritance
Will be a right-thinking, wise person or a fool?
Yet that person will get to use everything I worked for;
So it seems pointless to gather things that will not satisfy,
But will only be wasted in the future.

Lord, why should I go through all my hard work and pain?
Why should I use my wisdom, knowledge, and skill
To leave everything to someone who didn't work for it?
Even at night, my mind won't quit working.
All this work is pointless and meaningless!
Nothing is worth my work; nothing counts!

Solomon is not saying work is wrong or working for money is wrong. He is saying we should work to glorify God and in our work find the meaning of life. In this book Solomon is saying work without meaning is vanity.

Lord, Solomon came to the wrong conclusion
To eat, drink, and enjoy what one's work produced.
He thought that You gave food and drink
So that one could enjoy them;
He didn't realize we should all enjoy *You*.

Lord, the ungodly wastes his life collecting things
To leave to someone else after he dies;
Isn't this pointless and meaningless?
You give the good things of life to us,
But You want us to realize they came from You.
Amen

Ecclesiastes

CHAPTER 3
To Realize God Has Given Us a Time on Earth

Lord, all good things in life come from You.
There is a right time to enjoy the things I'm given.
We have our time to be born and our time to die;
A time to plant and a time to harvest.
We have a time to kill and a time to heal;
A time to rip up and a time to put together.
We have a time to cry and a time to laugh;
A time to grieve and a time to rejoice.
We have a time to invest and a time to reap dividends;
A time to hug and a time to stand off.
We have a time to hang on and a time to let go;
A time to keep and a time to give.
We have a time to rip and a time to patch;
A time to be quiet and a time to speak.
We have a time to love and a time to hate;
A time to battle and a time to rest.

Lord, what will I get from all my hard work?
I know You give us work to fulfill our lives.
You have given everything its time and place in Your plan;
You have made us aware that we're preparing for eternity,
But we can never fully understand what You're doing in our lives
For we don't know the beginning from the end.

So is it good to eat and drink and have a good time?
Is this your gift to me in this life?

Lord, I know whatever You do will last forever
And no one can add or substitute for things You do,
So we better fear You in this life.

Lord, that which was here when I arrived on Earth
Had already existed before I was born;
So You want a person to seek You
Rather than seek the elusive goal of happiness.

Lord, there is something else I observed under the sun:
I find wickedness everywhere justice is found;
I find justice everywhere wickedness is found.

Lord, there is coming a time for You to judge
the intentions of people,
Because You will judge both the righteous and the wicked.

Lord, Solomon said you were testing people by Your students
So they will realize they're not just animals.
After all, the same thing happens to people and animals alike:
They both die,
They both are buried in the ground.
Aren't humans better than animals?

We came from dust and we return to dust;
We are made in Your image.

Lord, does the sinner know what happens after death?
Doesn't he realize
The human spirit goes up and the animal spirit goes down?

Lord, the fact that I must die makes me search
To find happiness and meaning in what I do
In the allotted time You give me on Earth.
Amen

Ecclesiastes

CHAPTER 4
To Learn the Value of Others

Lord, Solomon thought about all the oppression
That was being done under the sun.
The oppressed were shedding tears,
And no one was there to comfort them.
The oppressors have the power to oppress
And no one is there to stop them.
The dead are happier than the living
Because they were already over their troubles;
Remember, the living still have to live with their troubles.
Does that mean the one not yet born
Is happier than the living that have troubles,
Or those who haven't had to face troubles?
Those not yet born haven't seen
All the evil that is done under the sun.

Lord, much effort and achievement comes because
One person envies another human.
Is this not pointless and meaningless?

Lord, fools do nothing but fold their arms
And reject the opportunities of life.
Better an armload of peace and tranquility
Than two arms full of pointlessness and meaninglessness.

Lord, there is another meaningless situation
When a lone person continues to work hard,

But there is no companion to share life.
There is neither son nor brother to come alongside,
As the person works endlessly for wealth.
He should ask, "For whom am I working hard?"
"For whom am I denying myself the pleasures of life?"
This is a pointless and meaningless way to live.

Lord, two are better than one because they work
cooperatively together;
If one of them falls, the other helps him up.
Woe to the one alone who falls;
He has no one to help him up.
If two people sleep together, they keep each other warm;
No one can be warmed by themselves.
An attacker can defeat the one who is alone,
But two can defend themselves;
A three-stranded rope is not easily broken.

Lord, a poor wise youth is better
Than a king who is old and foolish,
Who no longer listens to advice.
Even if the king has risen from the depths of prison,
He is poor when he will not listen to wisdom.

Lord, I have seen all who live and walk under the sun,
And I believe the wise but poor youth is
Better than the king who rules wrongly.
No matter how many subjects the king has,
Those who come after the foolish king
Will not regard him with reverence.
The life of the foolish king is pointless and meaningless;
His life is empty and nothing counts.

Lord, I'll be careful when I go into Your house,
I'll listen to hear Your voice and learn wisdom.
That's better than the fool who offers sacrifices,

183

But doesn't know his sins
For which he is offering the sacrifice.
Amen

CHAPTER 5
To Learn Tolerance

Lord, teach me not to speak too much, or be in a hurry;
May my words have meaning before You.
For You are in Heaven, and I am on Earth,
So I will speak only a few words.
Just as nightmares came from worrying too much,
So a fool is troubled because he talks too much.

Lord, when I make a vow to You, I will do it;
Because you reject the fool who doesn't keep his word.
I know it's better to not make a vow to God
Than to make one and not keep it.

Lord, I'll not let my words convict me,
And I'll not let church leaders say I made a vow
When I never made one.

Lord, I don't want You to be angry because of what I say
And destroy the few things I've accomplished.
Because everyone gets confused when there are too many leaders
Who claim to speak for God,
We ought to all just fear You.

Lord, when we see the poor oppressed and justice destroyed,
We shouldn't be surprised because judges don't always do right.
I know there's a higher power who will judge the judge;
And if not, God will judge all.

But the greatest place to live is where
The king makes himself a servant to the people.

Lord, those who love money never have enough money,
Those who love luxury never get comfortable.
When the number of jobs increase,
So do money grabbers who want some of the profit.
So the businessman's only enjoyment
Is to watch the parasites fight among themselves.

Lord, the working man enjoys his sleep,
Whether he eats a little or a lot.
But when the rich eat too much,
They don't sleep very well.

Lord, the worst evil is the man who hoards his money,
To hurt his life and business.
Another evil is misfortune to a father
So that his wealth is lost,
Then the father has nothing to leave his sons.

Lord, just as I came naked out of my mother's womb,
So I will go naked out of this life.
All the efforts to make money are nothing,
For I can't take anything with me in my hand.
As we came into this world, so we will go;
All my work earned me just hot air.
The worst evil is for a man with money
To eat alone in darkness, frustration, hurt, and in pain.

Lord, Solomon saw that it was good for a man
To eat, drink, enjoy life, and work hard,
For this is God's program for him under the sun.
If a man will accept his work as a gift from God,
At least he has something to keep him happy,
Nor will he complain that his life is short.
Amen

Ecclesiastes

CHAPTER 6
To Enjoy What You Have

Lord, Solomon saw another evil under the sun,
Some people have the power to get wealth and honor.
These rich people have absolutely no lack in life,
But they do not have power to enjoy what they have.
Then some stranger gets to enjoy what the rich accumulate;
This is a foolish evil in life,
It is pointless and meaningless.

Lord, suppose a man has 100 children and grandchildren,
And he lives a long life,
But he does not enjoy the things he has in life;
This is vanity of vanity – pointless and meaningless.
If that father could live and never die
It would be better if he were never born.
If a stillborn baby arrives in darkness,
And that child never saw the sun,
That child would have more comfort than
The father who does not know how to enjoy his children.

Lord, I work to provide food for my body,
Yet the appetite is never satisfied;
We always need more to eat.
Does wine satisfy the body more than food?
Is a person with experience better than a poor person?
Is it better for the eyes to see things as they are
Or should we desire the things in life we really want,

Not knowing if those things are good or not?
All our arguments are pointless and meaningless;
Life is empty and nothing matters.

Lord, whoever I am, I was named before I knew it,
And I know I am only human.
Therefore, I am not strong enough to defeat death,
Because it is mightier than any one of us.

Lord, there are many things that make my life futile,
So what can I learn from futility?
Who knows whether futile activity is good
Because it makes my life better and richer.
No one knows whether the activity is good or bad for a person
After he is gone in death,
So nothing is sure but a pointless, meaningless life.
Amen

Ecclesiastes

CHAPTER 7
To Have a Good Reputation

Lord, it is better to have a good reputation for all to smell
Than to have splashy perfume to cover up our stench.
And it's better to go mourn at a funeral home
Than go laugh at the movies;
For when you die, everyone will mourn your death
And say good things about you;
Because no one wants people to laugh at them.

Lord, grief is better for me than laughter,
Because sadness will make me improve myself.
In the funeral home I think a lot about life,
But fools do not think to improve themselves
When they spend all their time laughing.

Lord, I will listen to rebuke from wise people
Rather than listen to amusing songs by fools.
Because the laughter of fools is like thorns in a fire,
They crackle and pop but give off little heat;
The life of fools is meaningless and pointless.

Lord, if I get angry when people oppose me,
And I compromise my character by taking a bribe,
Is my life not meaningless and pointless?

Lord, the end of things is better than their start,
So I'm wise when I patiently wait for good things.

I should never quickly lose my temper,
Because only fools surrender themselves to anger,
And the fool becomes a slave to the feelings of the moment.
I never say the old days are better than today,
Because fools look at the beginning, not at the present,
Nor do fools look at how things will be.

Lord, help me get wisdom along with getting possessions,
Because both wisdom and possessions shelter me from hardship.
But better to have wisdom of the two
Because wisdom helps me keep possessions;
If I have things without wisdom, I'll lose them.

Lord, I know what work You can do;
Only You can make straight what is crooked.
If my life goes well, I should enjoy it,
But if my life becomes a crooked mess
Only You can help me compare my life to a straight line,
So I can do better in the future.

Lord, a lot of people do the right thing, but die young;
And a lot of wicked people live long lives.
So living right will not guarantee a long life,
Nor will living wickedly mean you'll live a long time;
God has a time when we'll die, so that's when we'll go.

Lord, I shouldn't stake all my life on just one rule
But I should live by all the right-believing rules;
Because I fear You who gives the rules.

Lord, wisdom can protect every area of my life,
Better than all the leaders of my city.
Because I am not perfect, but I sin,
Therefore, wisdom is my only protection
So I must believe-right and live-right.

Lord, I will not get upset when I hear someone criticize me,
Because I know I have criticized others.

Lord, I purposed in my heart to be wise,
But elusive wisdom seems always beyond my reach.
Why is it that things that are far away
Are more real than things close at hand?
This paradox is so mysterious I can't understand it.
So I search all the more to be a smart person,
I determine to know the reason behind things.
I want to know why the love of sin
Motivates fools to act so foolishly,
And they don't know how stupid they are.
So I realize life is empty and nothing matters;
Then, I discover there is a woman called death.
She is the trap than blinds us with blindness,
She puts chains upon our hands that were free,
She gathers us and drags us to her prison.
The one who fears You and pleases You
Will escape the woman in the final end,
But the sinning fool will be her eternal captive.

Lord, Solomon searched everywhere for truth,
He added one conclusion to another to find the answer,
But this was his conclusion:
Only one out of a thousand lives by wise-thinking rules,
But the woman death can no one escape.
You originally made people to believe-right
But most people think up insidious schemes
That will ultimately destroy their lives.
Amen

Ecclesiastes

CHAPTER 8
To Learn to Do What Is Right

Lord, who is a wise person who knows what things mean?
Sometimes I can see it in their faces
For their wisdom gives them confidence in life.

Lord, I will obey the laws of my nation,
Because this is what You want me to do.
I will not rebel against the goodness of my nation,
And I won't persist in breaking laws,
Because my nation punishes those who break its laws
And what the nation says is final.
No one can ask their nation, "Why do you have laws?"
But those who obey them will not be punished.

Lord, the right-believing person will know the right thing to do
Because it's always right to do right,
And those who do wrong will be punished.

Lord, people are greatly concerned over the future;
What can they know for sure about it?
Even when something surprises them
How can they know what is going to happen?
Just as no one can keep the wind from blowing,
So no one knows the future but You.
Death is the only thing we know for sure,
Even then, we don't know when we will die.
No one can escape the surety of their death,

Just as no one can pay another
To fight for them when they are drafted.

Lord, Solomon saw that those who brutalized other people,
Were taken to the church for a decent burial;
Those wise people who thought-right were cheaply buried,
So everyone forgot them when they left the church.
So it looks like everything that happens
In this life is pointless and meaningless.
Therefore, when punishment of evil is not carried out in this life;
Some people are encouraged to do more evil.
Even though the sinner can do evil 100 times and live,
But in the end days, things will go well
With the one who fears God.
But things will not go well with the sinning sinner,
Like a shadow in the fading sunlight
He can't prolong his days by anything he does.

Lord, Solomon couldn't understand why
Bad things happen to good people,
And good things happen to bad people;
It looks as if life is pointless and meaningless.

Lord, Solomon concluded it looks as if a person should
Eat, drink and enjoy himself
For as long as God gives him life under the sun.

Lord, Solomon became frustrated in his search for answers
That people's eyes can't see what they don't see,
That the mind couldn't possibly grasp
Everything that was happening all over the earth,
That even working hard to search out truth
One couldn't grasp all he observed,
That even the wise person who thinks he knows everything
Still doesn't know much of anything.
Amen

Ecclesiastes

CHAPTER 9
To Know the Difference Between Good and Bad

Lord, Solomon carefully weighed all the evidence
And concluded the life and death of the righteous and wise
Are ultimately in Your hands.
No one knows whether these people will be rewarded
With love or hatred in this life,
Because all options are possible to all.

Lord, the same things happen to the righteous and the wicked;
So anything can happen to anyone.
The same things happen to the good and the bad,
To those who confess their sins to You and to those who don't.
The same things happen to those committed to You
As those who are not committed;
The same things can visit any life.

Lord, the human heart will plan evil
As long as the person will live.
They live in their folly as long as they live;
Until they die, then their folly ceases.
There is hope as long as a person is alive,
So it is better to be a living puppy than a dead dog
Because the living knows one thing for sure,
They know they will die
But the dead don't know anything.

There is nothing left the dead can do
And all memory of them is gone.
The dead can no longer love, or hate or envy;
Every opportunity to do anything is gone,
They no longer share our life under the sun.

Lord, that means we should eat food and drink wine,
And enjoy what life we have on earth
For You know what we do.
Therefore, we should always dress our best,
Take a bath and look the best we can.

Lord, that also means we should enjoy life
with the spouse of our youth
In this pointless and meaningless life,
Because that is what we're supposed to do
In our allotted time in this futile life.
Whatever task is ours to do, we must do it with all our might,
Because in death there is no opportunity to prove ourselves;
In death there is no working, dreaming, or learning wisdom.

Lord, Solomon observed that races are not won by the swift,
Nor is the battle won by the strong.
Also he observed rewards don't go to the wise or intelligent,
Rather time and chance determine our life.

Lord, I don't know when the time will come for my death,
Anymore than fish taken in a net,
Or birds taken in a trap.
Death snares people at unfortunate times,
When it suddenly and unexpectedly visits them.

Lord, Solomon observed another unusual thing,
A king attacked a small town with few people.
He surrounded it with an army and many machines of war
But a poor but wise man saved the city.

195

No one expected the wise man could do it,
And after deliverance, no one remembered the man.
So Solomon says that wisdom is better than strength,
Yet the world pays little attention to wise people.
Doesn't this seem pointless and meaningless?
So we should listen to a wise man speaking quietly
Rather than jump when a fool barks orders.
Wisdom is better than the weapons of war
And one mistake destroys much good that's been accomplished.
Amen

Ecclesiastes

CHAPTER 10

To Learn Not to Make Mistakes

Lord, just as dead flies cause a good mixture to stink,
So does a little folly in a wise man;
And a wise man will follow his wise heart,
Just as a fool follows his foolish heart.
A fool does foolish things in his everyday life,
Showing everyone he is a fool.

Lord, I should keep doing my job when my boss gets angry with me,
Because calmness soothes an angry spirit.

Lord, Solomon observed another great evil under the sun:
When a leader promotes a fool to a higher job
And leaves a wise man in a lower position.
This is as foolish as a servant riding a horse
Making his boss walk.

Lord, those who dig a pit will usually fall into it,
And those who dig in a snake's nest will get bitten.
You will usually get hurt carrying stones too big for you,
Those who chop wood will get hurt with a dull ax.
If the edge of the ax is dull,
And you don't take time to sharpen it,
You'll have to use a lot more effort to chop wood;
Any wise person should know this.

Lord, a snake will bite if it's not avoided,
And the babbler will hurt you, if you hang around him.
The words of a wise person are always gracious,
But the words of a fool have a poisonous sting.
Because the fool thinks foolishly before he speaks,
He ends up looking stupid;
He just talks and talks, and says nothing.

Lord, the fool doesn't know what will happen in the future,
Nor can he tell me what will happen after I'm gone.
The daily work of a fool tires everyone out
Because he doesn't know what he's doing;
He doesn't know the way home!

Lord, woe to the people whose leader is a child,
Who starts the day partying.
Happy are the people whose leader had good training,
Who knows to eat at the proper time
In order to be strong for his duty.

Lord, when the owner is lazy, he has holes in the roof;
When he does nothing, there are leaks all over the house.

Lord, I know there's a time for parties and good times
And good friends add meaning to life,
And we need many friends to meet our needs.

Lord, I won't insult my leaders, not even in my thoughts;
Nor will I criticize my boss in my bedroom;
For a bird might carry my sarcasm to him
And I will suffer the consequences of my thoughts.
Amen

Ecclesiastes

CHAPTER 11
To Learn the Inevitable Consequences of Life

Lord, I will cast my bread on the water
So that I eventually reap a reward.
I will divide my investments into seven or eight places
Because a disaster may destroy one or two of them.
When a cloud is full of water
It will eventually rain on the earth.
Whether a tree falls to the north or south,
The place where it lands is where it stays.
He who waits on the wind will never sow,
And he who waits on the cloud will never harvest.
There is never a perfect time to do anything
So go ahead do what you have to do.
No one can predict the direction of the wind,
Just as no one can tell how bones grow in the womb.
No one knows how God does His work;
He is the Creator of the Earth.
Sow your seeds as carefully in the morning
As you sow your seeds at the end of the day,
Because you don't know what part of the field will prosper
Whether one side or the other, or if both will do well.
Then you will enjoy seeing what God will do,
And the working of the sun will give you pleasure.

Lord, if I live a long life
Help me enjoy all my days;

Yet remember there will be many dark days
That will seem to be pointless and meaningless.

Lord, if a youth spends his time only having fun,
If he only entertains himself,
If he does what's in his heart,
And does everything his eyes see to do,
Know that for all his wasted opportunities,
God will hold him accountable.
Therefore, don't be angry or sorrowful with what happens
Because you can't be young forever;
But what you do when you're young will stay with you forever.
Amen

Ecclesiastes

CHAPTER 12

Fear God and Keep His Commandments

Lord, we should all learn of You while we are young,
Before the evil days make our hearts hard;
We should learn before the days come
When we no longer have enjoyment in life;
Before our eyes become dim to see in the sunlight
And it becomes difficult to see by the moon and star light;
Before our mind gets cloudy when the sky is clear,
And our previously mighty muscles begin to tremble;
Before our backs bend with the burden of years
And we are no longer able to work around the house;
Before we begin to lose our teeth
And next we lose our eye sight;
Before we shut our mind to what's happening in the world,
And our ears can't hear what's going around us;
Before we have difficulty walking up stairs
And we are afraid of heights;
And when our hair is white like the almond tree in bloom,
And we can hardly lift ourselves,
And the aphrodisiac berry no longer helps.

Lord, when we are almost ready for our eternal home,
And our friends and family are waiting for their inheritance,
The silver cord of life is about to break
And the golden bowl is ready to crack;
So then we no longer draw water from the well of life.

Help us remember the dust of which we're made
As we return to join the earth,
And our spirits return to You
Who gave us life in the first place.

Lord, Solomon said life seems pointless and meaningless,
Nothing is worthwhile and nothing counts.
But, Solomon was wiser than his pessimistic conclusions
from his observations,
He researched and wrote out the principles of right-living

Lord, these principles for right-living are like sharp spurs
To prick our conscience when we do wrong;
And they are like bolts to anchor our soul
So we will have positive direction in life.

The preacher in his final conclusion now tells how to interpret his proverbs. His goads (called "spurs" in this translation) are the negative proverbs that a person must not do if they want to obtain the good life. The nails (called "bolts" in this translation) are the positives in Proverbs that he must follow if he wants to think correctly to attain a successful life, i.e., to understand and serve God.

The negative goad was to irritate the slumbering into action, just as a farmer prodded a sluggish animal with a sharp stick or goad. The fixed nail is a secure place where a man may hang anything, i.e., his clothes, weapons, or tools of work. These nails are principles that give the reader mental and spiritual anchorage. These are the preacher's "acceptable words . . . words of truth" (Eccles. 12:10).

Lord, I know many others will write books telling us how to live,
But we'll only get tired studying them all.

Lord, here is the bottom-line conclusion on how to live,
Now that we've heard everything Solomon had to say,
This is the answer to the apparent vanity of life.
Fear You, (God) and keep Your (His) commandments,
For this encompasses our obligation in life.

For You (God) will judge everything we do,
Including our hidden thoughts, whether good or bad.

The word order of the original text is, "God thou shalt fear" (Eccles. 12:13). The emphasis is on God, not on your emotions of fear or reverential trust. The fear of God is the foundational emotion that will tie all life together. Ecclesiastes says that man apart from God lacks holiness and pursues sin, but must face the righteous demands of God's holiness. God demands unquestioning obedience. Why? Because God will judge "every work . . . every secret thing."

Only in the New Testament can we clearly understand the judgment of God. We will find that only Jesus Christ is the wisdom of God (1 Cor. 3:21) and all of our motives will be judged (1 Cor. 4:5). All of the problems in Ecclesiastes point us to Jesus Christ who has the answer to every question.

PRAYING THE
SONG OF SOLOMON

To Learn the Meaning of Love

INTRODUCTION

Solomon wrote three books of the Bible plus some Psalms (1 Kings 4:32). He first wrote the Song of Solomon as a young man revealing true love. Second, Solomon wrote the Proverbs as a middle-aged man to reflect the wisdom for which he prayed, and the wisdom God gave him. Then after 1,000 wives and concubines, plus all the excesses of wealth, power, and luxury, he wrote Ecclesiastes as an old man to show the emptiness of possessions and power. The lament of Ecclesiastes is "vanity of vanities" (Eccl. 1:2). Apart from God, all is meaningless and purposeless.

Background

David had many sons; Solomon was not the oldest, so he was not first in line for the throne, but Solomon was God's choice to succeed his father as King of Israel (2 Sam. 7:12-17). The sons of David worked in the fields to learn character, just as David learned many lessons as a boy shepherd. In the fields Solomon met a young dark-skinned Shulamite girl, and fell in love with her. It was pure love! Suddenly Solomon was taken away to become king. She was left alone with his promise that he would return. She had dreams and desires, and as the old adage says, "Separation makes the heart grow fonder." She loved Solomon more in separation than in presence.

The day came when Solomon returned triumphantly to claim his bride. His chariot came dashing down the country road. It's described, "Who [is] this coming out of the wilderness like pillars of smoke?"

(Song of Sol. 3:6). The dust from under the chariot wheels are described as pillars of smoke, "Solomon the King made himself a (chariot), he made its pillars [of] silver, its support [of] gold" (Song of Sol. 3:9,10). It was a surrey with a fringe on top, "Its seat [of] purple" (Song of Sol. 3:10). Like a modern day teen with a "souped up" hot rod, Solomon came racing down a dusty road to get his "first love."

Solomon's mother, Bathsheba, is mentioned and apparently approved of the marriage, "King Solomon with the crown with which his mother crowned him on the day of his wedding, the day of the gladness of his heart" (Song of Sol. 3:11).

Characters

There are three characters in the Song of Solomon. First, Solomon the bridegroom is a picture of Jesus Christ who is married to the church. Second, there is the Shulamite, the bride who is deeply in love with Solomon. She plans to marry Solomon, but she doesn't always express her love properly, and is constantly seeking satisfaction in relationship to him. The third,character group is the daughters of Jerusalem, sometimes referred to as the bridesmaids, but others think they are the ladies in the court of Solomon. This group is called *THE CHORUS* throughout this translation.

Daily Quiet Time

The love of Solomon and the Shulamite is described as a garden, so it is like the place where the believer meets Christ. Throughout this book the daily quiet time with God is also described as a garden. The fulfillment of our intimacy is described in the metaphors of a pastoral scene.

Interpreting the Song of Solomon

When I wrote *Praying the Psalms* and *Praying the Proverbs*, I followed the basic steps that all Bible students take. The first step is to study the Bible itself to "see what it says." That means a student must master the facts of the Bible. The second step is to determine "what the Bible facts mean." This second step is called interpretation. Therefore, I wrote *Praying the Psalms* and *Praying the Proverbs* based on an interpretation of the text. I wanted my prayers to say the same thing that the Bible text says. The third step is to apply the Bible to our lives. This is called application. When you take this third step, you ask "what does it mean to me?" In the application, the reader applies the Scripture to his life. I wrote *Praying the Song of Solomon* differently. I didn't base it upon interpretation, but upon application. I first interpreted the book as I did other previous Bible books, then I applied the Song of Solomon to my intimate relationship with Christ. The interpretation of the Song of Solomon is to the purity of marital (sexual) love. But I didn't want to write *Praying the Song of Solomon* on marital love; rather, I wanted to write this particular book on our intimacy with knowing Jesus Christ.

Throughout the Old Testament, Israel was taught that her *Maker* was Jehovah the Lord, Who was her husband. Then John the Baptist came teaching that Jesus was the Bridegroom and we are the Bride. John said, "He who has the bride is the bridegroom" (John 3:29). Paul followed the same metaphor saying, "For this reason a man shall leave his father and mother and be joined to his wife, and the two shall become one flesh. This is a great mystery, but I speak concerning Christ and the church" (Eph. 5:31,32). Paul teaches that the union of the believer with Christ is a reflection of love in a human marriage. This is the spirit in which I've translated the Song of Solomon.

Just as a bride's desire is toward her husband, and she shares her heart with him, so the believer's desire should be toward Jesus Christ and the believer shares an open heart with his Lord.

Marriage intimacy leads to satisfaction, and that is one of the results of knowing Jesus Christ. Jesus said, "But whoever drinks of the water that I shall give him will never thirst. But the water that I shall give him will become in him a fountain of water springing up into everlasting life" (John 4:14).

The Daughters of Jerusalem

Many have asked who these young ladies are. Clearly, the daughters of Jerusalem are not the bride, yet they know her and are close to her. Notice what they know. First, they know where the bride is and how to find her. Next, they know where the bridegroom is located. And third, the daughters of Jerusalem continually point the bride to the bridegroom. They see his dignity, majesty, and love for the bride. The bride asks the daughters of Jerusalem to help her find her beloved. They help her because they want to see the bride and groom together. They represent the friends of the bride, i.e., in today's terminology, they are bridesmaids. Some have interpreted them to be the women of Solomon's court. However, they seem to be women from the Shulamite's home, so they are her bridesmaids.

209

The Song of Songs

What does it mean that this song is the "Song of Songs"? Does it mean that this was first written by Solomon? Is it about his life as a young man who fell in love with a girl he later married? Does it mean this song is the most beautiful or the most excellent of all songs? Or does it mean that this song is foundational to all other songs, i.e., that love is the basic ingredient of life? Is this the best of all songs because it's about *relationship*, i.e., relationship between Christ and us? He loves us deeper than a bridegroom loves his new bride, and we ought to respond in kind. Or, finally is it a song of excellence or literary superiority? This is the best song that has ever been written. Perhaps, the "Song of Songs" is about all of the above. This "Song" should be the song of your love to Christ.

Song of Solomon

CHAPTER 1

Giving Yourself
to the One You Love

Song of Solomon (1:2-2:7)

This beginning section shows the deep longings of a woman for her lover, and the deepness of her love is reflected when she is separated from him. Solomon, the son of King David, was given a job, as were all the sons of David. He was a shepherd, met a girl working among the vineyards, and fell in love with her. When David died, Solomon was abruptly taken away to become King of Israel. While Solomon was gone, she loved him all the more.

During this time the girl was criticized, saying Solomon would forget about her when he got into the palace. Her longing for Solomon is a metaphorical picture of the deep longings we have for Jesus Christ while we are separated from Him on this earth. We want to love Him completely, yet find ourselves living a finite life in a sinful world. People criticize the believer that Jesus will not come back for them.

The Shulamite found peace when she surrendered to her bridegroom, just as we find inner peace when we surrender to Jesus Christ. He becomes more than the King of our life, He becomes the object of our love who satisfies us, and fills our deepest longing.

Lord, this is the ultimate song of love
For it is a picture of our love for each other.

My Prayer to Christ

Show me Your unbounded love,
So I can experience Your intimacy.
When You said, "I will abide in you,"

You also reminded me, "You shall abide in me."
It's that oneness I want with You.

Lord, Your name is wonderful, it soothes me like ointment;
It heals my heart and relieves my pain.
This is why the young love You;
They want to experience Your presence,
They want to worship You in Your courts.

Chorus

Lord, we are grateful and praise You,
We will remember Your love forever;
It is the right thing for us to love You.

My Prayer to Christ

Lord, I am a sinner away from Your presence,
But I want to be a part of Your family.
Don't cast me away because of my sin;
I was born with a nature to rebel,
And I sin because of that nature.
Those who are sinners hate me because I seek You;
They have rejected me because I reject them,
But my home will no longer be their home.

Lord, show me again Your love; where can I find Your presence?
I want to rest with Your sheep.
Why should I have to search for You everywhere?
Why can't I come to Your flock?
Why can't I worship You with others?

Chorus

Lord, there are many of Your bewildered children;
They don't realize how close they are to You.
Show them the footprints of Your flock,
Let them feed from Your hand.

The Response of Christ

You are precious to Me as you serve Me;
As you serve others in the world, you serve Me.
Your face is lovely as you reflect My face,
As you look to Me, others see Me.
You will beautify Me as an ornament
Because you are the only way I am seen.

My Prayer to Christ

Lord, as You invite me to Your banquet table
Your mystic perfume draws me to Your side.
You are the One I love more than anything on earth;
I want You to rest in my heart.

Lord, You excite me as the smell of fresh flowers
Cut from the most desirable garden on earth.

The Response of Christ

Look at what you have in your heart,
You have the beauty of a divine nature.
Look—for you have spiritual eyes to see.

My Prayer to Christ

Lord, I can see with the eyes of my heart,
I see Your beauty...Your compassion...and Your strength.
I come to Your courts with thanksgiving,
I enter to worship Your majesty.
Amen

Song of Solomon

CHAPTER 2
Love Grows in Separation

My Prayer to Christ

Lord, You are my rose of Sharon,
Your fragrance and beauty enhance my life.
You are my lily of the valley,
You give color and tenderness to all I do.

The Response of Christ

Like a lily among the thorns
So I entered the pain of humanity.
Your thorns, the enduring symbol of your rebellion in Eden,
Inflicted My pain and drew My blood;
My love for all, my suffering, for the darling among humanity.

Song of Solomon (2:8-3:5)

There was a "forced" separation between the Shulamite and Solomon, just as there is a separation between Christ and us. Is this a picture of our working at our everyday job so we have little time for Christ? Is this a picture of the believer's trips into the world to satisfy the lust of the flesh or the lust of the eyes? Jesus, the Beloved, is not always present and the believer cannot fellowship with Him all the time. Yet, the believer seeks Him, wants to find Him, and show Him his love. The deepest of love is usually felt when the lover is absent from the one he loves.

My Prayer to Christ

Lord, You are the tree of life
Among the other trees of the forest.
You are the sustainer among all others;
I am peaceful sitting in the security of Your shadow,
Your life-giving fruit is sweet to my taste.
You bring me into your banquet hall,
Your banner over me is love.
You feed me with nourishment that no one else offers,
You give me satisfaction I could never find elsewhere.
You hold me close to Your heart,
You give me a purpose to live.

The Song of Solomon is a book of physical love, i.e. lying together, breasts, etc., however this is a statement not to stir up sexual excitement until a couple enters the marriage union. Therefore this key thought for the young is repeated three times: Song of Solomon 2:7, 3:5, 8:4. The phrase "stir not up," means don't get sexually aroused. The phrase "awake my love" means let your sexual passion lie dormant until you can fulfill sexual enjoyment in a biblical way, i.e., marriage. To modern youth, this is an appeal not to expose oneself to sexually explicit movies that excite sexual passion, and not to engage in physical touching that arouses sexual desire.

Chorus

We warn you children of Adam,
You must not awaken and stir this love.
It has its source in Jesus Christ alone;
Do not awaken or stir up your sexual love
But wait until your love is stirred in marital union.

My Prayer to Christ

Lord, I love to hear the voice of the One I love,
It bounds the boundaries of mountains;
Nothing on earth can drown out Your whisper.
You come to stand nearby, no matter where;

You come to look through the window of my soul.
"Come, my love, to Me." You bid me, "Enjoy your intimacy,
Near to Me, to know Me."

Lord, the winter has been barren, my soul is chilled;
I need the refreshing showers of spring.
The flowers smell so fresh when they first bloom in the warm sun;
The song of the birds excites my soul,
The sound of love comes from the dove.
The enticing bud is appearing in the fruit trees,
The grapevines promise new sweetness soon.

Lord, it's time to know You and to be known by You,
To touch You, O Lord, and be touched by You.

The Response of Christ

I am come to seek and save those who hide,
There are no recesses that I cannot find.
I will answer as you speak to Me;
I will be Your love...Your protection...Your all.

My Response to Christ

Lord, little details spoil my life, they demand my attention;
Yes, little details spoil the garden and take away joy.
Before the breezes of life make me old,
Before life's shadows lengthen into darkness,
Let me once more return to Your presence,
Let me feed until I am satisfied,
Let me talk to You until I've nothing more to say.
Amen

CHAPTER 3
The Fulfillment of Love

My Response to Christ

Lord, night after night on my bed, I sought to find You;
I looked everywhere for You, Lord, my Creator.
I tried every means to find You, but You were hidden;
You were not in the methods invented by others.
I got up from my bed, I went searching everywhere for You;
You were not in the crowds...offices...or in sports.
I frantically searched for You,
But You, Lord, were nowhere to be found.

Lord, I found men who guarded Your temple, "Where is He?"
I asked but they did not know.
Your guards abused me, they did not help me;
"How can I find him?" I asked the men.
They had not seen You,
Nor did they know where You were.
Scarcely had I left Your guards, when I found You;
I found You in the secret place of the Most High God.
"I will not let You go."

Lord, now that I know how to find Your presence,
I will bring You to my home;
I will tell those I love about my love for You.

Chorus

We warn you children of Adam,
You must not awaken and stir this love.
It has its source in Jesus Christ alone.
Do not awaken or stir up your sexual love
But wait until your love is stirred in marital union.

Song of Solomon (3:6–5:1)

The Shulamite got excited because the king came riding in his chariot to capture her as his bride. Solomon now has a crown, the royal chariot and soldiers to guard his every move. Even the daughters of Jerusalem recognized the greatness of Solomon. Thus, the Shulamite loved him more, and finds her delight in his presence, as he finds his delight in her. This is a picture of our abiding life in Christ and His abiding in us, "Abide in Me, and I in you" (John 15:4). This abiding life is one of fellowship, service, and satisfaction.

My Response to Christ

Lord, You came mightily into my desert wilderness
Where I am thirsty and dying,
Where I am lost and afraid.
You came in Your beauty and fragrance,
You came to enlighten my Spirit.
You came with the many fruits of the Holy Spirit
So I could eat and refresh my character.
You came with Heaven's finest to give to me
What I wanted to give to You.
You came with angels to protect me;
You faced the dangers before I knew them.
When I couldn't protect myself
You brought a wall of protection for me.

Lord, You have a chariot, it's the wind of Heaven.
It takes You where You go;
It brings Your majesty to be near me.

Your chariot is lined with grace, and drawn by Your power;
It dashes upon the path of mercy.

Chorus

You children of men, come see Your Lord, the King;
His crown of thorns is replaced by gold.
This crown gives Him authority over all born of women;
It's the crown given at the supper of the Lord.
Amen

Song of Solomon

CHAPTER 4
How Beautiful, How Wonderful

My Response to Christ

Lord, how beautiful are your feet that bring You to me;
How beautiful Your path that leads into my heart.
How wonderful Your eyes to see all that is,
That was, and that is to be.
Your eyes peek into my heart and You see my intentions;
You love me deeply in spite of my shallow love to You.
How magnificent Your words You speak to all,
But how meaningful what You say only for me.
Your message is a scarlet thread
That reaches from the throne of God to me.
I know Your lovely face my eyes have never seen,
But my inner eyes have memorized
Every line of Your features.
Therefore, I can say I know You—know You better than outward,
Because I've been behind the veil;
I've talked to You and You've talked to me.

Lord, in the early morning I will seek again Your face,
To be assured again of who I am.
In the darkening evening I will get myself
To the place where all my sins are erased.
I will come repenting...seeking...renewing.
Everything about You is beautiful;
You are my love and my God.

The Response of Christ

Come unto Me all who are tired and hurt,
Turn away from this earth's daily drudgery.
Come find your peace in My presence.
This world has many temptations, but I'll hold your hand;
It also has its dangers; I'll be with you
When it's dark and you don't know the way.
I was there in the beginning, to make all things new,
I'll be there with you in the future.
I am Alpha and Omega, the First and Last;
I am the One who is, who was, and who is to come;
The word of eternity is my breath, I am.

My Response to Christ

You are like a clear pool of water that appears to have no bottom,
A pool locked up; no one knows what is there
Nor do they know what will be, not even You.
You can be a fountain, a thing of beauty for all to see,
Or become a well to water the garden about my life;
Or by shutting it out, no one knows what You could be;
Not even ever—not even now.
Open Your pool to me, Your living waters give
Me a life that I never expected to gain;
Enrich me and others; everyone is so thirsty.

Chorus

Awake north wind! Come south wind!
Blow into the pool with beauty and life,
Let Him come walk on the waters, "Peace be still."
Amen

Song of Solomon

CHAPTER 5
Love Restored

Song of Solomon (5:2–6:10)

Something happened to the happy union. Perhaps Solomon got back to the palace and had too many duties, or he had to leave his bride alone for a day, or sometimes for more than one day. Their sweet fellowship was broken. Is this a picture of our lost fellowship with Christ through worldliness, or neglect, or some other sin that creeps in to break our fellowship to Him? Therefore, watch the focus of this section, it deals with restoration. Just as the Shulamite goes forth diligently to seek her lover, so we must diligently seek Jesus Christ after we have neglected Him. And how do we get full restoration? It comes when we search for Him with all our heart and then He reveals Himself to us and our communion with Him is restored.

The Response of Christ

I will come to you, entering the garden.
There will be fragrance in the morning vespers;
There will be sweetness in the evening watch.
Let us eat together the meat of fellowship.
Let us enjoy together the sweetness of honey.

Chorus

Eat, drink, as friends enjoy each other
More than the food that fills their stomachs.
Eat, drink, until you know each other intimately;
Until the moment is filled, and you return to earthly duties.

My Response to Christ

Lord, even when I lie down to sleep, my heart is awake;
I listen for Your voice when I can't see,
I trace Your form in the pages of my heart.

The Response of Christ

Open your heart to Me for I have words of love for you.
Look deeply in the Book of My heart,
There you see everything that was done for you.
Look again on the pages; don't stop where you begin.
You'll find it's not about your needs and wants,
Everything was created to glorify the Father.
The one thing He couldn't do for Himself, was worship Himself;
To do so is words already known.
I come to help you worship the Father, it's what He seeks.

My Response to Christ

Lord, I've removed my coat, must I put it on again?
My shoes are off, must I again put them on?
I feel Your presence come, but I don't know that You've gone
Until I feel empty and alone.
When I ignore what You want me to do,
When I am busy so that I don't think of You,
I open the door to You because of frustration;
But You are not there when I speak.
I thought You were everywhere in the world.
I sought You, but I couldn't find You;
I called out to You, but You didn't answer.
I was seeking You for myself...my frustration...my selfish need;
I was not seeking You for Yourself.
I went to the guards of Your Temple, I needed their help;
They beat me, they wounded me
They took away my joy, these guardians of Yours.

Chorus

I charge you all who would know Christ,
That you find the Man of Galilee.
Find Him for who He is, the Lord of the Universe;
Find Him for the love He has for you,
For the answer to lost love always begins with Him.
How can the Nazarene offer love differently from others?
Because beauty begins with Him.
For He has always been the source of love, He is love.
You learn to love by accepting it from Him.
How can His love differ from everyone else's?
When you take Him in your heart, you learn to give.

My Response to Christ

Lord, You are magnificently divine and wonderfully human;
You stood different than anyone else.
Your purity of love never changes;
It is only matched by Your changeless love of holiness.
It is we who change, because we are so hungry.
When we enter Your love, we feel Your acceptance.
When we get sidetracked...we stray...or we disobey,
It's then we experience the rejection of Your holiness;
You don't change, we move into a different light of penetration.
When we change, You wait in isolated solitude;
You say nothing new to us; You've said it all before
In the pages where we find out about You.
You wait lovingly...patiently...and expectantly
For us to come back to Your love,
For You did not change Your love to us.
It was we who spurned what we had enjoyed.

Lord, Your words are sweetness altogether;
You stand completely desirable.
But I tend to wander, it's my heart;
Take it and seal it for Your love alone.
Amen

Song of Solomon

CHAPTER 6
Unbroken Communion

Chorus

Do you know where your love is located
When you lose His presence in your life?
Do you know how to find your love
When you begin again to search for Him?
There is only one way we can help you find Him,
The answer is not within your loneliness.
The solution to every distraction and every escape
Is found by a renewed focus on Him.

Song of Solomon (6:11–8:4)

This is a section that describes the interactive love of Solomon and the Shulamite for each other. It is a picture of unbroken communion that is possible between Christ and us. It is a picture of our changed life when He lives in us, and we live in Him. What our relationship in Heaven will be like must be reflected in our fellowship with Him each day on earth.

My Response to Christ

Lord, I know You come each evening to the garden for enjoyment;
You return to the pool for refreshment.
You gather Your sheep at day's end and wait among the lilies;
You come to receive the worship that is due You.

Lord, I belong to You and I love You deeply,
And You belong to me.
Each evening I come to be refreshed in Your presence,
I come to offer You the love of my worship.

The Response of Christ

I am here each day, whether you come or not;
I come to receive your worship, whether you give it or not.
When you do not come to meet Me each evening,
It is not you alone who is neglected.
Yet, in your neglect, you do not strengthen your love
But allow it to be weakened.
But, I too miss that which I can't give Myself;
I seek such to worship Me.

I will be tender in your hour of brokenness;
I am compassion when you need My love.
But I am the Lord of Hosts, the leader of the fighting angels;

They are a formidable mighty army.
I have all power in Heaven and earth,
And I will be with you always, and all places.
March under My banner, stay close to My side;
There is safety from the god of this world
Who would terrorize you, then brutalize you.
Turn your eyes away from Me and you'll be overwhelmed,
But in My intimacy is security.

There are many who are numbered among Mine;
I have room for all who need and seek Me.
Throughout the years they have grown without number;
My rich love for each, I have for you.
But when we are together, give all of your love to Me
As I give all of my love to you.

When you become complete in Me, you find perfection;
  You and I exist as though there are no others.

Let others see you and say that you are happy,
  For when they extol you, they praise Me;
  For everything good in you is worship to Me.

Chorus

Who else shines brighter than the dawn?
Who else is stately...quiet...and lovely as the moon?
Who else is a warrior marching formidably before His army
  Inviting all to come under His banner?

My Response to Christ

Lord, I had gone to the garden, to meet my Love;
  I had gone to refresh myself in Your presence,
  To offer the fruit of my life in worship to You.
Before I knew it, I found myself swept up into Your chariot,
I was caught up in the excitement of atmospheric worship;
  I was in Christ and You were in me.
    Amen

Song of Solomon

CHAPTER 7
Come Back

Chorus

Come back child of Eve, come back often to Him.
Come back to see Him, come back to His presence.
Why are you looking around as though you're lost?
Why are you looking for the wrong things
In the wrong places?

The Response of Christ

How beautiful are the feet of those who come to Me,
How lovely the spirit of those who seek Me;
And how acceptable is their worship?
I am looking for those who weep because of their transgressions,
For those who realize the greatness of their sin.
I will listen to those who make a joyful sound
Of praise and worship and thanksgiving.
And if the sparrow is so comfortable it makes its nest
In the temple near the presence of Shekinah,
Why can't you go from trouble to trouble
To appear before My presence
In My house where I will meet with you?
Better one day in My courts with the Shekinah,
Than 1,000 days in any other house.
For I am your crown...your light...your water;

I am the dawn of life. See all things through Me;
No one lives except through Me.

My Response to Christ

Lord, I come to You; there is no other place to go
To find happiness and peace,
To enter life and enjoy life more abundantly.
I belong to You; I surrender my will to Yours.
Do with my life what You will.

Come Lord; let's use our evening hours to talk to one another.
I will tell You my concerns,
Then give You my praise and worship.
Arise Lord; let's meet each other early in the garden
Before the flowers blossom and merchants open their shops.
I will give you my love and receive in return
Your perfect love for me.
All kinds of experiences await us in the garden;
There is fruit to eat, flowers to enjoy,
Water for refreshment and fellowship to ponder.
I will give You that part of each day;
I will place You first in my life.
Amen

Song of Solomon

CHAPTER 8
Out of the Wilderness

My Response to Christ

Lord, You are closer to me than family
Because flesh and blood doesn't know the intimacy of the Spirit.
I will bring You to my childhood home to tell them all
That I have given my love and devotions to You.
I thank You for the lessons I learned from father and mother
For learning right and wrong, and regret.
If they had not taught me the importance of relationships
I could not reach out to You,
And receive Your presence.

Chorus

We warn you children of Adam,
You must not awaken and stir this love.
It has its source in Jesus Christ alone;
Do not awaken or stir up your sexual love
But wait until your love is stirred in marital union.

This section begins with the bride coming out of the wilderness, just as Solomon came the first time out of the wilderness. But this time there is a love relationship, "Who [is] this coming up from the wilderness, leaning upon her beloved?" (Song of Sol. 8:5). They are both together, and they lean upon one another. This is union and communion. Just as the bride is asking continually to be bound more firmly to Solomon, so we should attempt to be closer to Christ than ever before.

230

She is in the vineyard, like we in the secular world, more occupied with the beloved Christ than with the work that has to be done.

In this last section, the union-communion between bride and groom is now apparent; everyone can see their love, one for the other. She, like us, leans upon the Beloved. Why? Because Christ is our strength, He is our joy and He is the prize of our life.

The Response of Christ

You were not conceived by chance,
But I placed you in your family,
You were predetermined in character and temperament.
You were in My plans before the foundation of the earth,
I loved you eternally before time began.

My Response to Christ

Lord, set me as a seal on Your heart;
Keep me near You by Your strong arm,
For love is as strong as death.
Love flourishes as the flames of a fire,
And grows in intensity when nourished,
But melts when only one loves.
There is no water that can quench Your love;
Torrents of men who flourish hate have not put it out.

Lord, if a person spent all his money on love,
It would not be enough to buy love
For love is given, it can't be bought.

Lord, we are all human and selfish, it's impossible to give;
How can we gain Your love if we can't give?
We first receive what You give, for You give all,
And in receiving we learn to give back to the Giver;
As we give to You, we begin to love.

Chorus

Who is perfect? Surely no human can attain it.
But Christ came to give and a new nature to have.
He came to make perfect those who are imperfect
So we can all start perfect in His perfection.

Our Response to Christ

Lord, I am human; there is no loveliness in me,
So I come to you just as I am.
You have a garden, a place where You rest;
Let me tend Your garden,
A place where we can meet together.
Let me tend the garden with constant care
So that nothing can coax me from Your allegiance,
So I can retreat there when I need You.
Let me learn from Your presence; I will master it
So I know You perfectly,
And my perfection here will be as You made me perfect.
Let me cultivate prayer...praise...worship...and thanksgiving,
Growing myself to Your glory in Your garden.

Lord, my garden is mine; I can tend it as I please,
But I chose to prepare it for You
For my relationship with You is everything.

The Response of Christ

Who will live in My garden with Me?
Who will wait there for Me?
Who will listen for My voice?

My Response to Christ

Lord, I come to the garden alone, but suddenly You are there;
I find Your presence, and You find me,

And I am complete in You;
Be Thou complete in me.
Amen

CONCLUSION

Our Love for Christ

The Endearments of Love

The Song of Solomon is one of the greatest love stories in the world, so we expect many statements of love. The bride pleads, "Let him kiss me" (Song of Sol. 1:2), and "Draw me away!" (Song of Sol. 1:4). It speaks of the odor or fragrance of love and she calls him, "My love" (Song of Sol. 1:9). The ultimate expression of love is "to lie together," and he "lies all night between my breasts" (Song of Sol. 1:13) notice the contemporary phrase to "build a bed."

Those in love use symbols of beauty and fragrance to describe their love such as "she is called a rose...lily...and other flowers that bloom." These are phrases we use for Christ.

The Unsatisfied Life

Once the bride has fallen in love with Solomon, nothing else in life satisfies her. Her eyes have been opened to his beauty and she constantly longs for the full enjoyment of his love. "Let him kiss me with the kisses of his mouth—For your love [is] better than wine" (Song of Sol. 1:2). With true love there is always a desire to constantly enjoy the presence of the other. So it is with those who truly love Jesus Christ and find their pleasure in Him.

235

Once we fall in love with Christ, the world will never be the same to us, just as a couple falling in love will not treat other people the same way. Apparently, Solomon fell in love with the girl and visited her on occasion; even though those visits were short, they were precious times of enjoyment. Then, after they were separated, the memory of those visits made love all the more desired and real. That led to the fact that there is no real satisfaction when He is absent, so that those who have found abundant life in Jesus Christ are never really satisfied again with anything that the world has to offer.

The Constant Yet Occasional Interruptions of Love

In the Song of Solomon, as well as in true life, the groom is not always *with* the bride, nor is the person you love always with you. Just as the groom must go about his daily duties, so we cannot always be consciously aware of the presence of Christ. We have a job to do, children to manage, and problems to solve. The enjoyment of Jesus Christ between times of secular demands makes Him all the more precious in the interval.

Like an ever-changing tide, life has its ebbs and flows and so our walk with Christ has its intimate experiences and times of secular "chalkiness." We don't like it, but we can't always have the highest peak of pleasure. But that's life. Night must follow day, just as we see Him perfectly in the light, followed by times of sleep and separation.

"Let him kiss me with the kisses of his mouth for thy love [is] better than wine" (Song of Sol. 1:2 KJV). The Shulamite seems to be saying, "Were that his love were as strong as mine, and that he never withdrew the light of his countenance."

There is a love far stronger than resting. It's a love of always yearning, it's a love that seeks satisfaction. True love has an inner awareness that the other belongs to you and you to him. Even though Christ is waiting for us at all times, the greatest satisfaction to our deepest longing is knowing that He's in our heart and that every time we reach out to Him, He is there. Though we never rest in His apparent absence, we fully trust His presence in our heart, even when we are not experiencing our daily quiet time.

There is another thing about the bridegroom. She seems to claim Him fully, but she never fully gives herself to him. Love is obedience, and we don't always obey. The woman who claims to fully love the man, but retains her own name, has never fully given herself to the one

236

she loves. If she only promises to love and honor, does she really love if she has not promised to obey? Until love reaches the point of surrender, a woman will remain an unsatisfied lover and never find the intimacy in her husband that she needs. The woman who maintains control over her own things will never be content with the resources they must share equally and continually. She cannot claim her lover if she does not enjoy the resources that they own together.

So what's the answer to the unsatisfied life? Why do so many people go through life without real satisfaction? The unsatisfied life is really that the bride has more love for herself than love for him.

Because God wants us to understand our love to Christ, He has given us a human relationship between a man and woman. The problem of love is not with Christ loving us, it's with our accepting His love and returning His love. On earth, what would a prospective groom think if he knew his wife was having difficulty choosing him, or giving herself to him? That would be untenable to him—what must it be to our Lord?

So, God has built within the human heart the emotional separation between man and woman to teach us how to overcome the emotional separation between us and Christ. Only when our deepest longing unsettles us and becomes unbearable and we are driven to our lover, then can we find our fulfillment in love. So, we go through life unsatisfied, and do not experience love until we find our love in Christ.

And just as the bride must yield her very self to the groom—heart—hands—possessions—reputation—she cannot support the love he has for her, nor give love back to Christ, until she gives Him all.

We have all seen selfish brides, only wanting clothes to be pretty, only wanting money for things, only wanting the husband's obedience for control. How many women only want a husband for what he can do for her? Such a woman has not learned the true meaning of love; while she may give physical sex to him, she doesn't give him the love that satisfies his heart. So, the Church must learn to love Jesus Christ—we must properly express our love to Him. And how do we do that? By completely yielding ourselves to Him, whatever He may want.

The Morning Watch

We must take time to be holy! We should begin each day by quietly waiting before God, that way we will learn what to do, what to say, and how to respond to the problems of life.

When the bride finds her satisfaction in her groom—her king—she begins to find the key to life, "We will be glad and rejoice in you. We will remember your love more than wine" (Song of Sol. 1:4).

Nothing satisfies the soul like sacred and intimate communion with the Lord. You realize that He knows all about you, He understands you, yet He loves you still. That gives you strength to live that you've never had before.

When the Shulamite came into the presence of Solomon, she saw herself as she had never seen herself before. She confessed, "Do not look upon me, because I [am] dark, because the sun has tanned me. My mother's sons were angry with me; they made me the keeper of the vineyards, [but] my own vineyard I have not kept" (Song of Sol. 1:6). In the morning watch we have new eyes to see ourselves as never before. We see the mistakes of life, and we see the shortcomings of our actions. We see our sins and we realize the different ways we sin.

In the morning watch we realize the dangers of the day before us. Only in the presence of the King can we see the greatest danger of all, i.e., the danger of not loving the King with all our hearts. Our neglect of love to Him will lessen anything that we will do that day which we think important. It also lessens our ability to find our way into the inner recesses of His heart. If we are not watchful over our own souls, we'll end up powerless, and we'll become the maker of mistakes. Let us never forget that what we become in His presence is more important than the things we do for Him the rest of the day. When we abide in Christ, we come into His presence to tap into His life, then we give forth His fruit for the rest of the day.

Don't neglect to abide in Christ at the beginning of each morning. Oh yes, your groom will forgive you for not spending time with Him, but you wound yourself. When you're wounded often, you live a scarred life.

Restored Communion

The bride's heart quickens its beat when she realizes her lover is coming, especially if he is searching for her. Notice what she says, "My beloved is like a gazelle or a young stag. Behold, he stands behind our wall; he is looking through the windows, gazing through the lattice" (Song of Sol. 2:9). This is a picture of the groom enticing his lover. He doesn't reproach her because she has broken the relationship, but rather, he entreats her to come with him.

My beloved spoke, and said to me:
Rise up, my love, my fair one, And come away.
For lo, the winter is past,
The rain is over [and] gone;
The flowers appear on the earth;
The time of singing has come,
And the voice of the turtledove
Is heard in our land;
The fig tree puts forth her green figs,
And the vines [with] the tender
Grapes give a good smell.
Rise up, my love, my fair one,
And come away!
(Song of Sol. 2:10-13)

This is a wonderful invitation from Christ, Who desires fellowship with us, and He wants us to love Him as He loves us. The Man of Sorrows who died for us, can become the Man of Joys when we spend time in daily devotions with Him. Always ask yourself the question,

"What did Christ get out of my quiet time this morning?"

But as strong as Christ's love for us, He can come no farther into our heart than we invite Him. The same way, we can never go farther into His loving heart than we choose to go. Love is a choice, and the decision is ours to make. Will we love Him?

Surely you will love Him, you will go forth to receive His love. Surely, You will meet Him every morning. Because you are hungry you will want to eat the fruit that He offers. Because you are thirsty you will want to drink the Living Water. Because you are alone in this life you want His presence. Because you struggle with problems you want His solutions. But He waits in vain for us to come because we continue to struggle alone.

Little Problems

Every love relationship has little problems that destroy deep love. "The little foxes that spoil the vines, for our vines [have] tender grapes" (Song of Sol. 2:15). The enemies are very small, but they do a great deal of damage. When love blossoms, a little fox can eat it before it blooms. The blossom of love is but a touch, a kind word, or a note to the one we love. And do we express that same love to Christ in little ways?

There are numerous "little foxes" that run through the vineyard trying to destroy the love that is there. And what are little foxes but the little ways we please our flesh, the little evil pleasures we feed upon, the neglect of doing Christian things at the right time, and doing the wrong things during times of worship.

We are safe in Jesus Christ, and because we are safe, we take His love for granted. Wasn't that the response of the Shulamite? "My beloved [is] mine, and I [am] his. He feeds [his flock] among the lilies" (Song of Sol. 2:16). She felt that he was there any time she needed him. He was feeding his flocks among the lilies, yet, the bride didn't always enjoy his presence. Notice how lightly she turns him away; she doesn't spend time with her beloved. Rather, she tells him to go away; perhaps she thinks she could enjoy his love at a later time. She says wait, "Until the day breaks and the shadows flee away, turn, my beloved, and be like a gazelle or a young stag upon the mountains" (Song of Sol. 2:17). What a selfish woman, thinking she can find satisfaction in her selfish pursuits, rather than in her daily quiet time with her beloved. She tells him to be about his way, to go to the mountains and run like a deer; she tells him to wait until the evening time.

That's the same way we treat Jesus Christ. When we should have fellowship with Him in the morning we get busy with the challenges of the day, and don't spend time with Him. We promise that we'll spend time with Him in the evening, when it is cool. But does that time ever come? The bride who sent her husband away so she could do her selfish things discovered that the evening was different than she planned. At the end of each day the evening does come and she promised that she would be there when it was cool and when the shadows came. But notice what happened when she spurned his love. He was not there when she sought him. "By night on my bed I sought the one I love; I sought him, but I did not find him" (Song of Sol. 3:1). Sometimes when we turn Christ away, we don't find Him as eager to reveal Himself to us the next time we pray.

So then we must search for Christ with all our heart. We must go within our hearts to confess our sin of selfishness. We must confess our sin of preoccupation. We must confess our sin of neglect. So the bridegroom did not come when she called, but eventually his absence brought her back to reality. She said, "'I will rise now,' [I said,] 'and go about the city; in the streets and in the squares I will seek the one I love.' I sought him, but I did not find him" (Song of Sol. 3:2). Is it possible that she ran helpless around in the dark searching for Christ, when she could have enjoyed the presence of Christ in the early sunshine of the morning? The love she might have exchanged in the morning was not realized. Why? Because she neglected and told Christ, "No!"

When we run about in the darkness seeking Christ, where is it that we seek His presence? Notice what the bride said, "The watchmen who go about the city found me; [I said,] 'Have you seen the one I love?'" (Song of Sol. 3:3).

When we finally meet Christ in the quiet hour, we must confess our selfishness, and ask for forgiveness. Restoration is good. Any wife who has angered her husband knows the joy of restoration. God has provided the human restoration in the human marriage so we might understand divine restoration in our relationship to Him. "I held him and would not let him go, until I had brought him to the house of my mother and into the chamber of her who conceived me" (Song of Sol. 3:4).

Constant Communion

The most important thing in the Song of Solomon is the king—Solomon is the picture of Christ. It is Christ who has all power, He has all love, and He possesses all good things that He can give to us, His bride. Notice the bridesmaids were told to admire the king, "Go forth, O daughters of Zion, and see King Solomon with the crown with which his mother crowned him on the day of his wedding, the day of the gladness of his heart" (Song of Sol. 3:11).

Just as King Solomon was crowned, so we crown Jesus by all that we do and say to Him. We must be occupied with Christ, not for our sake. We glorify Jesus Christ by giving Him the worship of our hearts. We do not come to the quiet time just to cultivate our selfish feelings, but rather, we come to the quiet time for the pleasure of Jesus Christ. And to do so, we must admit that we usually enter His presence for our own sake, or at best, for the sake of praying for others in the church, or those who are unsaved.

When we make Christ the center of our life and we find that He is "all in all," then we know that He is the beginning and ending of everything. Then we begin to experience the exchange life, i.e., He lives in our hearts and we live in Him.

When we understand the true love of Christ for us, we become silent in our love for Him. We will not put Christ off as we have in past times. We will not neglect Him or send Him away. Rather, we will say with the bride, "He is mine and I am His." We want full restoration with Christ and with unbroken communion we hear Him say, "Until the day break, and the shadows flee away, I will get me to the mountain of myrrh, and to the hill of frankincense" (Song of Sol. 4:6 KJV).

When Christ forgives us, He cleanses us from every sin (1 John 1:7). We are declared perfectly righteous and He begins to change us into His image. It is then that Christ says in the words of Solomon, "You [are] all fair, my love, And [there is] no spot in you" (Song of Sol. 4:7).

It's wonderful to know that our beloved Christ can be satisfied with the human love that we give to Him. That should motivate us to accept his invitation and offer our love to Him in the quiet time each day. We should go there seeking His presence, wanting to tell Him of our love for Him. Notice what Solomon said to his wife, reflecting the words of Christ, "You have ravished my heart, my sister, [my] spouse; you have ravished my heart with one [look] of your eyes, with one link of your necklace" (Song of Sol. 4:9). The phrase, "you have ravished my heart," can be translated from the original, "you have given me courage." It is interesting to realize that Christ's heart can be encouraged by our fidelity, companionship, and expression of gratitude.

Denying Any Recognition

It is interesting that the bride loves Solomon and wants to have happy fellowship with him. The daughters of Jerusalem (bridesmaids) call to the Shulamite, "Return, return, that we may look upon you!" (Song of Sol. 6:13). There's no question that she is the bride, and she has the bridegroom. But when the bridesmaid wants to see her in her beautiful gown, she is no longer concerned how she looks, or what she is wearing. She is concerned only about the bridegroom. And just so, we must be concerned about Jesus Christ who is the object of our love.

Some see in the word "return" as an indication of the rapture of the Church, and that might not be a wrong interpretation. However, let us remember that Jesus said, "'Surely I am coming quickly.' Amen. Even so, come, Lord Jesus!" (Rev. 22:20). The important thing each day is Jesus, and the important thing in the future is Jesus. We should not glory in our bridal gown or the fact that, as the bride in the ceremony, we are the focal point. The most important thing is Jesus, the Groom. The bride asks the question, "What will ye see in the Shulamite?" (Song of Sol. 6:13 KJV). She doesn't want any attention for herself. Just as Moses came down from the mountain unaware of the fact that his face shown because he had been with God, so we leave our quiet time each day, unaware of the fact that our spiritual face shines because we have been with God. And the important thing is not that our face shines, but that we have been with God. The important thing is that others will see the beauty of Christ in us—they will see our face shine with His glory.

Additional copies of this book and other book titles from DESTINY IMAGE are available at your local bookstore.

Call toll-free: 1-800-722-6774.

Send a request for a catalog to: